CONNECTED!

CONNECTED!

::

How #platforms of today will become apps of tomorrow, and how to #connect and create an exceptional #CX in the new world order

MANISH GROVER

CD Press
Competing in Digital

Connected! How #platforms of today will become apps of tomorrow
Author: Manish Grover, www.manishgrover.com   Publisher: CD Press, www.CompetingInDigital.com   Book website: www.manishgrover.com/connected
First Published: 07 Apr 2017

The publish date of this book is special because April 7 is my father's birthday. Dancing The Digital Tune was published on Nov 2, my mother's birthday. Dedicating these works to them is a way to acknowledge their profound inspiration and influence on me. Special thanks go to Saritha and Arya who invented time to help me write. They embraced whole heartedly the many absent minded encounters.

ISBN: 978-0-692-35873-3 (paperback) 978-0-692-35872-6 (hardcover)

To Arya and Mirai, architects and builders of the future

And to mom and dad, whose journeys inspire my own

GO ONLINE!

Use the below QR code to go to the book website and also access the list of references online:

http://www.manishgrover.com/connected

CONTENTS

WHY CONNECTED!

The promise of the future is that the world will be connected. But it won't be just about developing platforms. In fact the platforms we are building today will be inadequate to drive customer engagement and commerce of the future.

Why is that? It's simply because our customers are human, and connected. In fact, the focused and specific platforms of today will become components of much larger platforms. These larger interconnected platforms will logically arise as a result of collaboration between innovators and their individual platforms. They will connect with each other to complement their own capabilities, and probably also try to compete with one another. The big difference will be in how the logical platforms allow creation of context and value.

As the world changes, we need to create a place in the new order of our customers' minds. The frameworks in this book will allow you to do exactly that. These include extending customer personas and customers to beyond our own channels and products, creating a 3-Tier loyalty model, engaging customers in context of an ecosystem, and integrating not only all of our own value propositions, but also those of other companies across industries. Finally this book contains 3 important mechanisms for executing successfully on the promise of a connected world.

How #platforms of today will become apps of tomorrow, and how to #connect and create an exceptional #CX in the new world order

BACKGROUND

::

The buzz today is around building the platforms of the future. When I started writing the outline for this book in the winter of 2015, I hoped to write about Customer Experience (CX) and the Internet of Things (IoT). These were both heavyweight topics in today's digital, connected world. Several books have been written on both these topics separately. But just like the goodness of most great things is enhanced by putting them together (think cake and ice-cream), I decided to consider CX and IoT together because they are almost meant to be; with an underlying foundation of digital and data of course.

But then, I ran into a slight problem. Those of you who've read my first book - *Dancing The Digital Tune: The 5 Principles of Competing in a Digital World* – will recollect that the ultimate vision I laid out is about moving away from isolated products and campaigns, and move towards an ecosystem. Advances in technology have made it possible for consumers and customers to access what they want, on the go. What's more, industry boundaries are crumbling with every company trying to be all things to all people, and disrupting established business boundaries. Amazon is thinking of becoming a transportation and grocery company, while almost everyone is trying to become a bank.

So I had to make a choice. Either I could maintain an arm's length from this technology revolution that is bringing companies together, or I could make it an integral part of this book. In the end I chose to expand the scope because it'll help you uncover a very potent mechanism to create the customer ecosystem you desire. That technology revolution is the concept of APIs (Application Program Interfaces). It is through APIs that modern internet works. So as you read through, keep in mind that a focus on APIs, CX and IoT will help you achieve this vision of how we would like to play tomorrow's game. In addition, various technological and business process advances – including digital, data analytics, mobile, virtual reality, augmented reality etc. - can be grouped under the term "CX" and IoT so we can maintain our sanity.

It is critical to think in terms of ecosystems because that's the only way we can dominate customer engagement, or at least be prepared to ward off attacks from predators. For the sake of maximum impact, this book uses and presents possibilities. It doesn't just list and describe what others are doing. Instead of stories of glory, I'll find and present frameworks that will hopefully guide your travels and imaginations. The world is changing rapidly and almost all industries are undergoing massive shifts in their business models. How we engage with our customers and suppliers, and how they will in turn interact with us is changing dramatically. Some business models will be disintermediated, some will manage to hang on, while some will surge ahead.

Therefore, to make this book useful, I decided to not make it about listing and describing a bunch of these potential disruptions, or even showcasing examples from the market while leaving you to determine the best way forward for your organization or product. Instead, the intent of this book is to interpret the developments, and then systematically build an actionable framework that can comprehensively address these disruptions as they evolve.

This book is about helping you build a practical, top down model that you can get started with implementing immediately. I also recognize that there are many approaches to realize the intended goals of building a customer centric, efficient, technologically advanced, and well-oiled machine. So using heavy technology jargon or specific technologies would just not be the best use of this space. It will leave you guessing and confused. So I decided against doing that. Instead we'll discuss reference models that will help you quickly adapt them to your scenario, and get started with execution.

First, if you are reading this book, you are aware that IoT (Internet of Things), APIs and CX is set to transform many industries. We've often defined IoT as a lot of devices talking to each other. But you will see that IoT is about more than that. I expand the definition. IoT now includes analytics, interpretation of customer journeys, and bases the conclusions on data from all devices, not just from those devices that are machines (e.g. not just your Fitbit, the Apple Watch or washing machines but also from your mobile phone apps and the businesses you interact with – including your car mechanic!). For the business practitioner looking to truly leverage CX and IoT, the benefits are from cost savings and revenue growth potential. Customer experience, cross sell, operational efficiency, collaboration and customer engagement are all subsets of those two broad areas. Advances in CX and IoT mean that activities such as customer service, contextual targeting and promotions, healthcare, insurance, and field service of equipment, are all influenced heavily. The simple fact that information previously manually entered and collected is available and actionable in real time is a game changer. Patient health monitoring, remote equipment monitoring, customer location awareness, connected cars and trucks, are a few of the everyday examples.

Second, this connectedness means that business models - the ways in which we make money – are changing, often dramatically. The expected norms of customer engagement are disappearing and leading to new players and new ways of making money. We no longer have to stand on the curb for a taxi, no longer have to go into a branch to apply for a bank account, no longer have to clip coupons for our shopping, no longer have to hustle for cash to share a meal with friends, and no longer have to send in physical health forms to our insurance company. In fact, at your kids' schools, you probably don't even have to consciously pay for their cafeteria expenses! (I'm still grappling with that last one for so many reasons). In fact, we may not even need to buy a car soon.

These developments open up significant opportunities in our customer engagement models, as well as in how we look to compete as a business in the new economy. But more importantly, we can also easily see the huge gaps in the way we are engaging our customers. Almost all of these changing scenarios include the customer. Whether we have a customer whose machine we are automatically fixing, providing new billing methods, trying to get them to connect their car to the internet, sending them promotions on their phone based on their location, shipping them groceries, getting them to renew a subscription, or whatever it is we might be wanting them to do, there is a customer or user involved. Their experience matters, as we strive to improve share of mind, retention and sales of our products and services.

The point is not that we are now changing. But instead it's a question of "how" we are changing the way we engage. Instead of using technology to just put the old wine in a new bottle, we need to transform how we engage, not just leverage the new technology.

Think about these aspects when you think about the old wine in a new bottle:

1. *Our customers expect us to help them make the right decision. That's different from expecting us to sell to and push them to buy.*
2. *Our customers expect us to make their transactions simple and cost effective for them. That's different from providing the best product, but making it a nightmare for the customers to get it.*
3. *Our customers expect our advertisements to actually match their in-person experiences with our brands. Traditionally we've used branding (with some exceptions) to get top of mind recall with no linkage to how the customers actually use the product (or discard it).*

Our customers are under a siege of independent offers, value propositions, new channels and new products. And this flood of interactions is driven by predictive analytics fueled by our ability to gather more and more data. However, the future is about connecting their needs and addressing them without the need for extensive predictive analytics. If we don't, we'll be playing the same old game with new tools.

As the world changes, we need to create a place in the new order of our customers' minds.

So this book helps begin this journey with the big picture in mind. Those who will jump in first with a seamless, connected experience will forge ahead. The frameworks in this book will:

1. Outline what it is exactly that makes for next generation customer experience
2. Define what our new CX platform will look like and how it might play with others
3. Define a Rubik's cube of interlocking capabilities
4. Allow us to naturally think of ecosystems in everything we do

The age of Connected and contextual experiences is here. What we need now is to get away from anecdotes and begin to take this very seriously and systematically.

Individual stories do not a strategy make. So it's time to put all our eggs in the same basket (or something like that).

Let's go.

INTRODUCTION –
THE PLATFORMS OF
THE FUTURE

::

In the age of the machines (it's almost here), Customer Experience (CX) will be defined by how machines talk to machines, how machines talk to humans, i.e. us, and how humans talk to machines. It's a little jumbled up but the bottom-line is that we will be somewhat like Tom Cruise in Minority Report – initially confused and totally at his wits end, but ultimately coming to grips with the fact that there will now be activities and actions we just won't initiate. We are learning to give up control and hoping that the machines do the right thing. And a large part of that collaboration between machines and organizations will be through digital technologies and APIs, based on data that will be enhanced by IoT.

The Car Has Graduated

Tesla has beaten Google – and arguably everyone else - in bringing the first autonomous driving car to the market. Actually, that fact is irrelevant for us. What's more important is that previously long standing human interaction models – owning a car, servicing the car, and navigating the car – are now almost obsolete. What's even more important is that our sloppiness and carelessness is now giving way to a much more systematic method of maintaining our assets. It also means that auto insurance will take on a new meaning. There won't be driver errors to insure against because there won't be any drivers, and hopefully no accidents. And just like our Windows machine gives us notice to reboot or lose our work, the car will now take over its own maintenance.

Our car will finally be capable of pulling its own weight. The car can finally act like a grown up instead of us having to fuss over it like a baby.

On the one hand, there is the technology side of the story where connectivity, data and algorithms are making it easier to let machines finally take care of themselves, and free us to do more important things like sit on the front seat and nervously bite our nails. That's the promise of the Internet of Things (IoT) and a connected world.

And on the other hand is the Customer Experience (CX) side of the coin. Beyond a nice gentle voice, and pulling over when it's updating itself, or storing some favorite destinations, how does the car of the future cope up with the customer experience (CX) aspects? How will it know that I'm running a little late for my son's piano recital, but my wife has me covered so I can take the detour to a gift shop? Or that I need to pick up something from the grocery store on the way home? (PS: Assume for now that stores still exist.) And more than that, how will that information feed into the many car rental services that are likely to come up as the case for car-ownership dies.

Does the car really even need to consider these scenarios outside of its core purpose? After all, we have an "app for that!"

The answer is that the car of the future is like the future of software. And the future of software is platforms, not just programs meant to fulfil a specific business use case. The platforms of the future will be multi-purpose and multi-user, providing capabilities, not functionalities. They will be "plug into" and play. Different platforms will connect with each other to complement their own capabilities, and probably try to compete with one another. So, just as your phone is slowly turning into a platform, the car of the future will also act a platform. The car of the future will rid us of the need to look at many different apps and help bring them together in a meaningful way. Other businesses are coming up with their own platforms – retailers, banks, manufacturers. The future promises that all these platforms and networks will be connected seamlessly to each other. The network of platforms will be meaningful, and the single, platforms of today will be apps that feed into this network of platforms.

Smile and Please Open Your Wallet

Have you ever been to a bazaar where small merchants and sales people constantly approach you to sell you stuff? It's nice to be the center of attention for a while, but no matter how colorful and useful the merchandise, all that attention soon starts to get on your nerves. And that's before you realize that you're just being taken for a ride. You develop the thick skin and the right attitude to ward off the charging pests. Think of all the junk email you receive. It's the same noisy environment, right?

Now let's cut to back to your home in your favorite, peaceful, suburb or perhaps to your apartment if you are in a city. Till recently, a public place such as a mall or a retail store were places where you could re-energize, be a little lost, and explore without having to stave off charging sales people. It wasn't a bazaar.

Not anymore. The advent of Smart Signage means that a camera sees you walking into a store, captures the emotions on your face, evaluates your demographics, and then gets down to the business of selling you as best as it can. The dialog starts with coupons being sent to your mobile and instructions on how to find an item in the store. You even see the same offers when you get on Facebook, or are reading your favorite blog or browsing online news. After all this, if you still don't respond, the conversation starts becoming a little more personal and threatening with messages that tell you to "buy now or lose the offer forever" (yeah, right). And then your primal instincts take over and you switch off your phone.

Of course, it's not all bad. We love it when selling and promotions are helpful like when a store tells the associate to show us the dress from last time when it wasn't available in our size. Or when your bank can help you keep within budget during the holiday season. And that's precisely how CX and IoT are two sides of the same coin. The systems in the store are part of a platform now. They are probably going to connect with your car soon, and they are already connecting with your bank, your Facebook account, your Pinterest activity, your phone service, and trying to create magic for you. A lot of those connections are happening through digital interfaces and made possible by APIs.

The key, however, is to create meaningful magic.

Tourism Redefined

Perhaps one of the biggest changes in the way we travel is being brought forth through the concept of experiences. I would have thought the largest hotel brands in the world would do this first, but its Airbnb that is leading the way. By offering up what they call "be an experience host", they are indirectly helping travelers plan their destination experiences in addition to just managing a room.

After all, most of us travel to travel. Indeed some of us travel to just get away from the madness of our daily lives, but we all would love to experience our destinations in full. Soaking up local customs and cultures, getting to know the history, enjoying the food, checking off the high profile touristy things (of course) are all on our wish list in our own unique way. Before life got so crazy in this digital world, it was both a pleasure and a pain to plan a vacation. Now it's almost a nightmare to cut through all the noise, and be satisfied that we have the best possible plan.

In *Dancing The Digital Tune* in 2014, I thought it would be Four Seasons to blaze this new path. But it's Airbnb that has cut through the noise by offering up experiences. The travel industry is in for a huge change if they will care to adopt and embrace this change. The traditional landscape of a multitude of tour operator sites and social media blogs is taking on a new avatar. This avatar promises to evolve into a new kind of platform: a place where local merchants will finally have an equal say in a contextual manner. The platform will not be driven by everyone clamoring for our attention, but be singularly focused on the outcome desired by us – plan and make our trip memorable and enjoyable.

It will be important to not think of this future platform as a marketplace. Instead, personalization and context will be used to help drive our core purpose forward. Instead of providing us more and more options, this customized experience will narrow our options, and help us decide, not just make us decide by throwing so much information at us that we make a sub-optimal decision. What's more, this interconnected platform will allow for advisors – middlemen will be forever – to help us cut through the noise and plan the right experiences for us.

What's more, my hypothesis is that the pioneers such as Airbnb and Uber will become mere players on this larger platform, in addition to running their own platforms like everyone else. Why? Because this new platform will be based on a customer's end to end need, not just a transaction. It's a race to dominate tourism, or at least be relevant in the age of platforms. The Internet of Things (IoT) will probably be the medium as it tracks and automates, and premium will be paid for the best Customer Experience (CX).

Taxi! And it Won't be Uber or Lyft

A lot of us have forgotten what it is like to wait on the curbside and hail a cab. It was not romantic, not secure, and definitely not very convenient when it came to making payments, be rewarded for patronage, or arrange transportation in remote places.

Lyft and Uber changed that forever. I do think it was a little unfair to drivers who have been locked into membership of traditional taxi companies. Drivers paid top dollar for the privilege of operating a taxi, and now that privilege is useless. But that's not the topic of our discussion here.

What's more important is that this revolution of Uber and Lyft is about to end. When platforms will be more oriented towards customer's end to end use cases, the dominance will reduce. When I fly, my United Airlines mobile app allows me to get a Uber cab at my destination. That's because the traditional taxi companies have been busy fighting the wrong battle. The true battle is that of being in places where their customers are. As more and more taxi companies open themselves up in the same fashion that Uber did, will United be able to keep up with displaying all these options on their mobile app. Not likely. And as customer look elsewhere for this flexibility (customers are weird when it comes to choices), this might cause the utility of the United mobile app to decline. That will automatically open up the demand for a new aggregator. That aggregator will now be the conduit to many different transportation companies, including Uber.

In fact, the point of entry may be the interconnected travel platform I described in the previous section, bringing us back to a democratic platform world. We can expect the same to happen on every individual platform that companies might launch. The nature of this web of platforms will be described throughout this book. As you read this in 2017, all this may seem like complete guesswork on my part. But the movement to that connected, nebulous, autonomous platform is happening, that's for sure.

The beauty is that you can see it evolving but you won't be able to define an owner.

The Smart Industrial Machine

GE is really leading the marketing for the "industrial internet", their term for the adoption of connected machines. As a manufacturer of machines and equipment, GE has realized that connecting the machines so that decisions can be taken in real time when stuff happens is the future. And if they don't do it, they'll be left behind.

In addition, GE is going one step further by developing commercial software to tap into the power of connected machines, even if the machines are sold by someone else. This software will monitor the machines and alert owners when actions need to be taken. These actions can either be:

1. Predictive so that actions be done in anticipation. For example, a machine whose sensors report some data that upon statistical analysis signals failing ball bearings. Left unchecked, the eventual failure of these bearings can cause expensive damage to the entire machine. So a technician can be sent over to check and replace those bearing before they fail.

2. Break fix repair– when a failure is detected, we know of it already. So before a customer needs to call us, we can proactively take action and call the customer.

So what's the catch?

Even in the so called "Industrial Internet", machines will not work in isolation, and will eventually have to interact with each other. A boiler in a factory may have to speak to the safety system, or the sprinkler in the garden will have to speak to the owner of the car that is standing right next to it. Someone, somewhere, will have to build that communications layer. In fact, if we look beyond the industrial use cases, embedding the customer demand pieces into the equation increasingly make sense too. For example, supply chains are no longer expected to operate in isolation. For at least a couple of decades now, producers and suppliers have been trying to predict how much they should make or ship. What's better than connecting their supply chains to the demand side of the equation? Think of how our car manufacturers are allowing us to personalize our cars, so they can order and ship just the right car. For some reason this simple CX and customer engagement technique hasn't caught up with the advanced digital players in retail and banking.

Maintenance and efficiency is priority, but without embedding themselves into the customer ecosystem, disruption and obsolescence for the smartest of machines will be quick. In addition, how these actions are taken will determine – and will be determined by – the customer experience we wish to provide or are required to provide. This customer experience is going to be pretty complex to manage. There will be many different software platforms from many different manufacturers, each designed for a great CX, but together they might get on the customer's - or the technician's - nerves. A less than optimal CX will also be a massive deterrent to the cause of the connected industrial world.

Summary

The examples I discussed in the previous sections are not far-fetched. The rate at which we are moving, it will probably be wrong to just assume that they are. Things are in such a state of fast paced change today that nothing is impossible. The future will be based on sharing and communication. Monopolies of today will beg for share of market tomorrow as platforms will evolve to be larger and centered on end to end use cases. Platforms will have to interact with each other.

My tall claim is that underlying all these platforms will be contextual triggers and not prediction algorithms. The future is one-one customer interaction which will dramatically reduce the use of mass analytics as it is used today. The age of collecting and making inferences from mass data to drive next best offers will give way to contextual dialog with individual customers. The race for data collection will become streamlined because we will know what data we want and how we want to use it. The future will be about assistance, not selling. Those who sell and expect customers to determine a fit with their needs will be cast aside. Because in a connected world, customers will have little patience for the wild guesses we are throwing at them. The backbone of this connected world will be the interconnected platforms. The success of each individual competitor will be determined by the quality of contextual customer experience they provide. In other words, if a platform doesn't share, it will be cast aside.

My tall claim in the previous paragraph is based on 2 broad areas.

- First, think of a service – or a combination of services - as our personal assistant. Do we expect our assistant to interrupt us every time or ask permission for everything. That would be a nightmare. Some things just have to be done. For example, my map software asks me multiple times on a road trip if I want to accept a faster alternative route. That's both dangerous and annoying, not to mention potentially illegal too with changing laws. The list of these instances can go on and on if we sit down and make a list of interruptions in our daily life right from ordering detergent, calling a cab, to playing music, to paying our bills and so on.

- Second, given that services start taking action independently on our behalf, the use of artificial intelligence will become a lot about reassuring us that the things are getting done the right way, most of the time. AI will also be about learning new factors that lead to decisions. Considering the same example above, my map software should take the alternate route unless there is a reason not to (or tell me it is doing so unless I don't want to). And my bills will automatically be paid based on my payment patterns and if I have enough balance to cover other expected monthly payments. Artificial intelligence will be increasingly used to determine potential triggers that may cause a deviation from the usual. That's a much better way of creating seamless customer experiences. It's not perfect yet, but customer adoption of such features is already increasing in every industry.

The promise of the future is that the world will be connected. This implies that the platforms of the future cannot be about individual products and services to be sold. They have to be about the customer, and about fitting into the broader ecosystem. It's not likely that individual platforms will operate independently on their own, regardless of the number of retention barriers they create. Innovators will always find holes, and the baggage of legacy inertia will raise its ugly head without regard to our glorious past, no matter how recent that past is.

You might wonder about how this will all happen? How will the transactions at a retail store be mapped to what you bought at the coffee store, or to the kind of car you drive, or to where your next vacation is? That's actually the easy part. Data sharing, gathering and processing is becoming easier and easier. It's more a matter of the right privacy controls and how we think strategically to make our plays. It is extremely important for businesses to find out how they are going to play in this connected world.

It may sound like utopia to know everything about the customer. But the real challenge is about letting go of our traditional sales and marketing instincts. Think about it. When everyone has all the information, how does a customer decide amidst all the noise? Why would a customer choose you over others who are probably selling the same thing and probably at the same discounts?

It's Deja Vu. It seems like the same pitch battles of more promotions, more discounts and more noise that we've been getting used to over the past few years.

In the connected world, those who think that the battle is about making the most noise at the right time will lose. The platforms will need to have 5 key characteristics if they hope to win. I introduce them in the next chapter.

THE FRAMEWORK FOR CX IN THE CONNECTED AGE

As I outlined in the previous chapter, unprecedented innovation is underway today. Everywhere you turn there is data, and there are services and products to help you make sense of the data. Less typical are methods today to put those insights into action but they are evolving too.

The buzz in our lives and in the marketplace is palpable. We hear every day from visionaries, innovators, adopters, doomsayers and naysayers. Some claim that the Internet of Things is the 4th revolution that will disrupt the world (agriculture, industrial, internet, and now connected). Others are making technologies such as blockchain usable and realizing large valuations in the capital markets. Still others are looking to adopt connected devices into their businesses to make operations easier, and provide engaging customer experiences.

On the other hand, we have doomsayers and naysayers who speak of risks, while they nevertheless enjoy the technological advancements in their daily life without even being aware of how their every activity is now being tracked.

However, it's time to think of a framework for CX in the connected age. Without a consistent framework, the returns on our investments will be insufficient to match the effort we put in.

As you read on, keep in mind that it will be a big mistake to consider any of the innovation categories such as digital, analytics, IoT, automation, blockchain as independent developments. The industrial internet will soon be linked directly to the consumer internet, and both of them will inadvertently trigger massive business model changes. If you wondered at how household names such as Nokia and Kodak disappeared in the previous decade, then you'll be amazed at how many more such brands will fight for survival within the next few years.

Let's start with a story and then lay the foundations of the framework from there. The framework for CX we will develop in this chapter will help us develop the right technology, business and organizational capabilities in order to compete in the connected world.

Two Friends – a Lion and a Mouse

There once was a lion who was basking in the warm sun in a jungle, when he felt something climb up his tail. From the corner of his eye he noticed a small mouse who had mistakenly wandered towards him, and wasn't aware of the trouble it was going to get into.

The lion kept still as the mouse made it way over the lion's back, and all the way to the neck when it realized what it had gotten into. But before the mouse could run away, the lion used its great paw and landed the mouse right in front of it. And as lions do, it engaged in a game of "try to escape if you can" with the mouse, before it would eat the mouse.

Finally the mouse gave up and decided to make a plea to the lion. "O lion," the mouse said, "I am really sorry I bothered you. I have a family waiting for me at home. If you let me go, I promise that I will come to your help when you need me. I will be your friend." The lion laughed. "You will help me? That will never happen. You're lucky I've had my fill today so I'll let you go. Go home to your family and count your blessings.".

The mouse ran home. Several months passed and he did not see the lion again. Then one day as he was enjoying a warm summer afternoon with his family, he heard a roar. And then another. It sounded like the same lion he had met a few months ago. And he seemed to be calling for help. "I'd better see", the mouse said to himself. And he climbed out of his hole and looked in the direction where the roars were coming from. Sure enough, he saw the lion caught in a hunter's net unable to get out.

Quickly, the mouse ran over to the lion. And using its sharp teeth he cut through the net just as the hunter was approaching. The lion managed to escape to its safety, with the mouse on its back.

And that's how the mouse and lion became friends.

Why Customer Experience is Not Just Your Problem to Solve

What was the purpose of the story about the lion and the mouse? It wasn't a perfect example but I hope it helped to understand the context. In a quickly converging world, we are reaching a point where industry boundaries are merging. And how we strike up the right partnerships will decide the success or failure of our enterprise. Previously unrelated and often competing industries are going to be working very closely together.

This obviously means that the model for customer experience and engagement is crossing new frontiers. Visiting a fitness center in New Jersey, I came across a health insurer that rewards people if they exercise regularly. Preventative healthcare is big today, especially as insurers find new and innovative ways to reduce redemptions and claims, and then hopefully, our premiums. Initiatives such as these on connected customer experiences provide a huge jump in customer engagement. What's more, these relationships are a win-win for both parties. The fitness center has more customers who are more engaged because they have something more to hang on to than their New Year resolutions. On the other hand, the health insurer has a customer base that is arguably healthier, or is at least pursuing healthier habits. In addition, both businesses now have more avenues for engaging customers in conversations. This collaboration to motivate people in new ways is important for customer engagement. We all know from personal experiences that sheer willpower or desire is not enough to keep most of us straight with our fitness goals. It takes a strong event, or even an external force, to make us do what's right for us. And similar to the scenario in this case, businesses can work together to create win-win arrangements or customer journeys.

The exploration of new and innovative models such as these opens up immense possibilities. For example, an obvious extension of this model could be a food supermarket (online or otherwise) partnering with either the health insurer, or the fitness center, or both, to create tailored shopping lists. This can then extend on to dietitians, delivery services, and even with health professionals to advice and craft the right total fitness regimes.

The list of businesses that can get engaged with each other to create a win-win for their customers can go and on. And while this seems far-fetched, this reality is not too far away. Back in 2014, a bank in Russia had tied up with fitness centers to rewards customers with additional money in their savings accounts if they exercised regularly. The advantage for the bank of course was greater engagement with customers, and more active, higher balance carrying accounts. Recently we have seen new innovations such as Apple's Siri, or Amazon's Alexa or Microsoft's Cortana, being able to perform many different kinds of requests for users. These voice activated agents can connect to many different websites and services to order pizza, check the weather, check us in for a flight, query our bank balance and so on.

All these are examples of how companies are already coming together to realize innovative ideas, and linking them with social advancement as well.

Some of the characteristics of these new CX programs are obvious:

- They create multi-party benefits by tying together the business drivers of each participating entity.
- They provide increased CX – Customers have a higher, more tangible interest in adopting these programs because customers get more for their investments.
- They are social friendly – If the rewards are provided a non-monetary flavor, customers and members will share them more actively, resulting in excellent promotion on social media
- They provide an automatic loyalty program – If various tiers are created on engagement then there are multiple automatic loyalty ladders that can be created – one for each business.

The Plenti program by American Express is an excellent example of how they were able to create the world's first cross-industry and cross-company loyalty program. Moreover, the structure of the cross industry collaboration that is outlined in this section goes a step beyond even Plenti's innovative industry program: *The connected model without a single underlying broker links businesses and customers together by bringing benefits that customers would find hard to buy with money.* Loyalty is also the subject of the 2nd building block of our *Connected!* Framework.

The Connected! Framework

Customer engagement and experience capabilities have a far reaching and profound impact into our organizations. We cannot not change how we work, and how we think, and still expect to be creating magic with our customers. So the framework that I am outlining in this section provides a simple and immediately actionable blueprint to begin making progress. The framework in this chapter forms the basis for the rest of this book. We start with realizing the essence of what a digital, connected model means, and then we support that ambition with a roadmap and required primary capabilities

Without further ado, here's the overall model that we'll discuss and elaborate throughout the book.

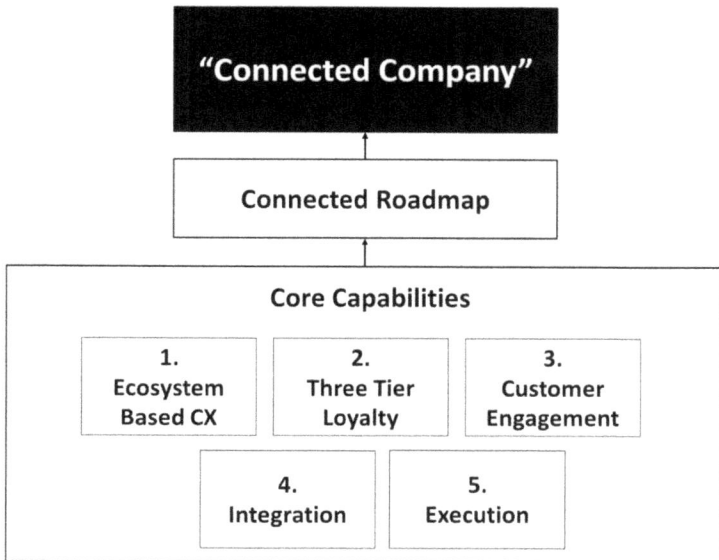

Fig: The Connected! Framework

What is a Connected Company?

The subsequent chapters on the connected roadmap and each of the 5 building blocks will dive into great detail on individual capabilities. However we still need the big picture of what this is all about. The vision of a connected company comprises of both a philosophy and a physical manifestation.

The philosophy of being a connected company relates to an expansion of what we consider as boundaries or limits of our products and resulting customer experiences. As the several examples we saw earlier in this book demonstrated, physical boundaries between industries are falling as it becomes easier to share and process real time data. So measuring ourselves on digital capabilities for distribution and access to our products alone is an approach that is strikingly inadequate to create engaging customer experiences of the future. We must instead look at the entire customer engagement ecosystem. That in turn implies that we think of our products portfolio as just one of the vehicles to drive customer engagement with our brand.

In addition, the entire concept of digital maturity assessment has changed for the purposes of defining organizational direction and strategies. While individual portfolios and channels can still apply the traditional definition of digital maturity and what it means to be an early mover, innovative player, or a digitally advanced powerhouse, those parameters are no longer very useful in defining overall competitiveness. To summarize, *digital strategy is not about our digital capabilities, but instead it's about defining how to compete in a digital world.*

A connected company thus operates from the outside in. In addition to taking products to market, it builds a broader customer context based on value propositions from external products and services so that it has multiple entry points into the customer ecosystem. Further, a connected company consistently reinforces these customer engagement entry points through a culture of advice and channel integration. We've already seen some good examples of companies that have initiated their journey towards being a connected company. Blue Cross Blue Shield of New Jersey partnering with Lifetime Fitness was a great example. A more traditional example is the marketplace that Amazon provided to its vendors. The marketplace has since become a defining force in fueling Amazon's own ambitions as a retailer of various services. The Russian bank rewarding customers for physical fitness activity is another example of how companies are moving to an outside-in philosophy. While there are still several capabilities these firms have yet to build, they have chosen the right path to the future.

On the other hand, the physical manifestation of a connected company is about how it operates and brings the connected philosophy to life. As you would expect, one of the first characteristics is to be able to bring its own products together as per the spectrum of customer needs. Any organization that has grown organically has portfolios of products that complement each other, or are related in some way. And each of these portfolios is based on customer needs. A connected company defines its structure in such a way that the focus of its go to market is on the customer, and not on the individual product portfolios. For example, sales training and incentives aligned on customer benefits, branding or marketing messages that support sales, alliances or partnerships to support the branding, digital channels that offer advice first, loyalty that aligns with customers' goals, etc. These capabilities result in a dramatic change from the inside-out culture of organizations. Inside-out organizations pinned the success of their channels on first order measurements of sales and brand awareness. While those metrics will remain as the ultimate yardsticks, measurement of the means to get to those metrics will be different. Take cross sell for example. We place a lot of emphasis on ensuring that customers purchase multiple products and services. To achieve this result we implement various programs and incentives to ensure collaboration among various business lines. In the connected model however, the customer centric approach automatically presents these various business lines as tied together in logical ways. No new cross sell is needed. In addition, the success of cross sell is now perhaps linked to those external value propositions that open up additional entry points into customer engagement. For banking, these could be travel, or retail, or education. For professional services, these additional entry points could be products from manufacturers upon which services are based. The crucial difference in the connected model is that the attention has to shift to address the entire customer needs spectrum. In turn it follows that internal processes and hierarchies have to dramatically adapt and change.

How a connected company will come to life will be examined in detail as part of the 5 capabilities we will explore in the following chapters. For, now, suffice it to say that the physical manifestation will depend on how a connected company defines its philosophy. I cannot emphasize enough that the philosophy arises from the premise that *digital strategy is not about our digital capabilities, but instead it's about defining how to compete in a digital world.*

The Fundamentals of the Connected Roadmap

Traditionally a roadmap for digital strategy has been focused on experimentation of innovative approaches, piloting them, building a supporting and aligned organizational structure, rolling out actual business process innovations to parts of the business, and measuring results in order to validate assumptions and define future investments.

While a general model like this still applies, the parameters of innovation and the means to measure success are dramatically different. The primary differentiating factor surfaces from two observations.

First, it is increasingly obvious that in the future, businesses will not operate in a silo. Instead, falling industry boundaries are mandating that we start to explore partnership models that focus on customer engagement, and look beyond traditional distribution or product partnerships. This new way of looking at our business strategy automatically changes the entire landscape of how we view innovation and customer engagement. This new lens exposes many new models of building customer journeys, engaging them, and measuring success.

Second, as the new version of customer journeys start to get developed, the platforms we are trying to build will take a dramatic turn towards being only a partial piece of the puzzle. This requires a huge change in mindset. If you think about it, creation of the current platforms has not required a change from the "build a destination portal" mindset of the mid-2000s.

Although the channels and means to reach customers have evolved, we still rely on building traditional retention tools such as loyalty and discounts. New product categories of a disruptive nature have evolved in the form of Airbnb, Lyft and Uber, and Amazon, but each player now relies on momentum and more-for-less, rather than sticky customer engagement. In short, the platforms that these players have built will be superseded by the fact that they will be mere players in the new order of things. These platforms will instead become mere apps – existing to fulfill demand if they continue to operate in silos and don't take steps to build cross-industry collaboration and customer journeys. The new platform of the future will become a nebulous ecosystem of participating platforms and apps. That nebulous platform does exist today in the form of various actions a customer - or sets of customers - takes to meet their needs. The only difference is that the platform doesn't show itself. As we move forward, the nature of that overarching platform will become more tangible and obvious.

So the connected roadmap that we will explore in the next chapter will be comprised of three aspects:

1. **Opening up:** Instead of cordoning off our products and services, how do we open up to other players in the industry who can help the customer with adjacent needs, or lead customers to us.

2. **Originating transactions:** Building a customer engagement layer that will help us originate transactions not only for ourselves but also for our partners.

3. **Connecting Value:** Leveraging the intelligence we are building to move beyond just predictive analytics and guesswork, and instead move towards a conscious

engagement with customers across multiple players in the new overarching platform (not just our own platform or products)

The Building Blocks of the Connected Roadmap

The 5 building blocks bring focus to the practical and executable aspects of being a connected company. Long term visions need to be supported by quick wins that move us closer to the end goal. Each of these 5 building blocks will outline short term, as well as more complex long term capabilities. This hierarchy of capabilities will serve multiple purposes – they will enable validation of the ideas, they will enable refinement of the ideas, they will engage and build a community of advocates both inside and outside the company, and they will show success that will allow more resources to be marshalled towards the longer term vision, thus accelerating the journey towards being a connected company. Each of the 5 capability blocks is needed to be a 'connected company'. The capabilities are interrelated and we cannot hope to execute towards the longer term goal on just one of them. Although we can certainly demonstrate quick wins on each of them and thus add fuel to the growth engine to build momentum and force.

- **Block 1**: The concept of Ecosystem based CX shows us how we should be building customer journeys that span not only our channels and products, but instead focus on the customer and leverage the power of our ecosystem. This means that an inside-out customer journey that shows customers interactions and touchpoints with our channels and products across the purchase lifecycle are no longer adequate. We must look outside in.

- **Block 2**: The 3 Tier Connected Loyalty model will outline how the concept of loyalty has to tap into customer aspirations and motivations and how to extend the loyalty and rewards model to span the connected ecosystem. This chapter also demonstrates how to improve the cost of redemptions while adding greater value to our customers.

- **Block 3**: The connected model of Customer Engagement shows us how emotional and physical engagement touchpoints should and can complement each other. It also shows how to reinforce customer confidence in our brand so we can become a reference anchor in our customers' minds by being an advice engine.

- **Block 4**: The connected model of Integration is about how we present ourselves to our customers to build lasting and meaningful customer relationships. It will show us how we need to unify the combined appeal of all our products and services. In addition, this capability will show us how to extend the value of our portfolio by bringing the power of our ecosystem to our customers.

- **Block 5**: The Execution capability will perhaps clarify the biggest challenge facing leaders today – how to execute and thrive in a new connected world. This block combines various techniques and outlines practical methods to get going and build on the momentum. We will explore the concept of creating and leveraging a new structure I call connected communities, what a CX focused organizational design looks like, and how the traditional concept of the balanced scorecard model should be adapted to turn our companies into connected powerhouses. I introduce the connected scorecard that will tie things together.

Now that we have a blueprint of what it means to be a connected company, let's move forward on this exciting journey.

The Connected Roadmap

Now that we've outlined what a connected company looks like, let's define a roadmap of sorts to reach the goal of becoming a connected company. While I'm going to present the capabilities as a series of stages, the roadmap should actually be considered to be more like a Rubik's cube of capabilities that flow into each other to help realize the vision of the connected company. The term *connected* has many different flavors – customer experience, technology, partnerships, security, privacy, interoperability, analytics, innovation, and the list goes on. Our goal is to build a set of capabilities that link us tightly to the customer's overall need.

Let's first quickly look at some pieces of the puzzle that need to be put together, or understood for us to really start thinking about building a connected company.

Technology Conundrum

Technology and budgets are different for everyone. And technology is one of the most powerful enablers today. However, it is not easy for everyone to start building around, or on top of their existing technology platforms. Indeed, platform providers would have you believe that they have the full stack of capabilities you will ever need to do everything that you might wish to ever do, to meet everything that your customers can ever desire. How wonderful that would be! But of course it isn't. The promise of the future is plug-and-play in ways that can never be met by monolithic technologies alone. As you read through this roadmap, think of interactions with other businesses, not just your customers. And focus on customer context as people, not just your customers.

Business Engagement – Old Wine in a New Bottle

To our customers we claim that information asymmetry is disappearing. But asymmetry is actually causing us to miss the big picture when it comes to the real business capabilities that will matter in the long run. In fact, a majority of the conversations about next generation technology is about opening up access and develop APIs. And almost all platforms are striving to meet that need by thinking of new direct channels. But isn't that like serving the same old wine in a new bottle. Opening additional channels for acquisition is important but channels themselves don't drive customer engagement. In the new connected world, leading with channels for transactions represents the old way of doing business. In fact, by building non-technology intensive tools that engage customers and build context, we might far exceed the gains from a new channel. For example, it's great to have a button on a retailer's website allowing your customers to query and apply for credit. But when we lead the customers to the retailer with the credit already applied for (or analyzed), we create even more impact. Opening up access to commoditized services might help in the short term by creating new channels but the real question we should worry about is customer engagement.

The Whirlpool of Data – Putting the Cart <u>before</u> the Horse

Analytics and data is all the talk today. And it's easy to get sucked into the whirlpool - we don't have data, and we don't know how to analyze it, so we need to do that first. But in a highly digital and connected world, have we ever wondered that predictive analytics is merely going to be an operational effectiveness enhancer, not a game changer? Customer relationships built on intimacy do not guess about their customers. Instead they already know each other. Think about it for a second. If I already knew what my customer needs, would I have to guess? In fact, I would argue that we have the privacy debate in reverse. We have a privacy debate because we have a customer engagement problem, not vice versa. Data and analytics are useful. However for a connected company they will be about improving operational effectiveness, not about finding what our customers need. Reflect on that for a second.

The reason this discussion on the roadmap – or Rubik's cube - is so important is that we are moving very rapidly towards a connected world, and in ways that are changing the industries we know at their core. Every day there are new innovations in the ways we serve our customers, new types of partnerships we create, and how we expand our own services to encroach upon a space that was designated for someone else. All bets on what a core business is are off in this digital world. Regulation might slow down the change as it mulls over the issues, but it won't prevent the change. In fact, regulation will adapt to the change more quickly than we think it will. We've already seen that in case of taxis, hospitality, online retail, and now banking.

The most important takeaway is that we can no longer take for granted our position in the industry ecosystem. Whether vertical integration of services makes sense or not, the fact is that in the short term the trends are strong enough to push a strong incumbent into oblivion if we don't keep our guard up, keep evolving, and be ready to take quick action.

Here's how the roadmap or Rubik's cube look like.

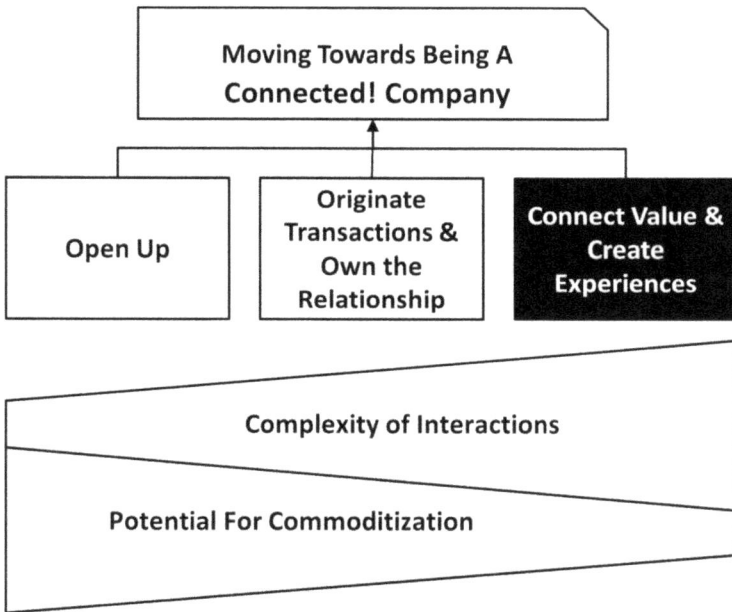

Fig: Moving Towards Being a Connected Company

The various items spread across the three steps of the roadmap can be adopted in ways that suit a specific institution's needs. All we need is a clear idea of the goals.

One of the many ways to be ready for this massive industry evolution is to start thinking of opening up and be ready to embrace new business and operating models. The connected roadmap presented here will help assess our current state in this journey, and our path to evolution. The checklist of capabilities mentioned as part of the roadmap phases are not new or pie-in-the-sky items. Most of these are already being used increasingly by digital first companies in various ways.

The 3 stages and various checklist items should be seen as a Rubik's cube. As we solve for the end state, different parts of the cube will come together. And they can be approached in many different ways. For example, the first stage is to open up API access to third parties. But to make strong and rapid headway, we might instead want to adopt parts of stage 2 first to start engaging customers much better through various interactive tools and trying to understand the full context of their personas.

Level 1: Open Up (Provide Access to Core Services)

The obvious mantra for the connected world is to have the ability to be embedded into the places where our customers are. To think of this simply, consider that customers should be able to use our services from outside of our physical location, website or mobile app. As I mentioned before, doing only this will be akin to serving the same old wine in a new bottle. But this is a critical capability to have if we are play in an open ecosystem. The next two stages will put more color on this evolution so for now let's focus on understanding this better.

What does the spectrum of opening up access look like? Some common use cases and categories are:

Browse and Inquire	Education & Purchase
• Look up product information based on filters • Check eligibility based on demographic, location and income information	• Apply and get approved for product/service • Buy product and associated services • Combine offers and deals in context depending on where they are provided
Service	Supporting
• Include transactions into the related post-sales processes • Provide service status and	• Allow experience to be tailored by channels (e.g. white labeled, or co-branded)

updates on the account lifecycle (e.g. statements, payment due dates, renewals etc.)	• Allow for capture and use of preferences • Allow independent access as required • Allow for use of marketing automation • Provide usage reports and analytics • Provision for cross sell / up sell

Here are some examples of specific use cases:

Retail

- Locate stores
- Check pricing
- Review inventory
- Place order
- View delivery times

Banking

- Check balances
- Make payments
- Check bills that are due
- Review and analyze transactions
- Apply for a new account
- KYC

Manufacturing

- View catalog

- Place order
- Trigger maintenance
- Shipping and delivery alerts

These use cases are not an exhaustive list by any means. They are meant to illustrate how technology is helping to change the way we interact with our customers, our partners, and our channels. A significant percentage of new services and products provide this functionality already. Especially in the service providers and payments space where access to a core service is critical.

- Payment services such as PayPal, Authorize.net or Stripe can be embedded anywhere a payment can be made from. For general banking, there is still a lot of potential to make progress
- Many common commerce functions such as shopping carts, personalization, advertisements are provided as a service
- Card Linked Offers platforms allow for retailer promotions to be available to bank customers, and they are increasingly personalizing the offers as well
- A bank offers services such as Bill Pay that are made possible through integration of many 3rd party software providers
- Retailers are building capabilities to often send your receipts to a safe provider of your choice so you can manage warranties better. In fact, a hackathon by Deloitte focused exactly on this problem using a new technology called blockchain (see ref 17).

Every day the models of integration and customer experience are being made much broader. The intent of opening up access means an improvement in customer experience. For example, a recent innovation by a bank in this evolution is Wells Fargo's integration with Xero, a SaaS accounting service provider (see ref 18). Customers of the accounting software would previously have to download and import transactions. Now it is just a one-click (or few clicks) action to gather the banking account data in context. This kind of integration was already in place with PayPal and Intuit for example, but Wells Fargo is one of the first banks to do so. What's the advantage? Xero benefits because it provides a unique advantage and ease of use to customers who have an incentive to stick to Xero, or subscribe to it. Wells Fargo benefits because they offer one additional reason for small businesses to stick with them, and flock to them.

It is common for SaaS (Software as a Service) organizations to open up and provide access to their core functions, but in the digital age, this capability is becoming critical for everyone. As we've seen before, voice services from Amazon, Microsoft and Apple are able to interact with airlines, taxi services, retailers, banks, and many others to perform services in real time for the customers. That's a huge step forward in contextual fulfilment of needs. Similarly, software that gets embedded in popular chat services such as Facebook Messenger, can execute the same service requests without us having to leave the chat window (see ref 19). These are all examples of opening up access to our core services. As retailers such as Costco and Walmart start getting into financial products and insurance, it is crucial for other businesses such as banks to step up and compete with new digital capabilities of their own. And one of the easiest ways is to open up and provide access to their products.

What are some of the feature set considerations while opening up services for digital consumption? There are 3 aspects that help plan for optimal customer experience:

Tiered Access and Permissions

Just like Facebook allows you to determine which application can access your data, the collaboration between businesses should also be able to provide control over who can access, how much can be accessed, and when can it be accessed. And it should be easy for customers to review and modify this information.

In fact, management of data privacy and permissions is set to undergo a huge evolution as the data of your customers will not be yours alone. Surprise! On the one hand, governments are stepping in. The payments regulation in the UK (PSD2) has made it clear that banks don't own the data they have of their customers, and they must make it available to others (see ref 20). Imagine if that happens to retail? On the other hand, customers would like to be paid when their data is used to add to our bottom line (profitability), or top line (revenue). Ever wonder why your smartphone manufacturer, retailer, or search engine provider shouldn't pay you for using your data? Sure they are providing a service for free in return, but that probably won't be enough given the benefits being driven by the snooping that's about to take place in our private lives.

Context

Understanding where the user is, and why the access is being made or requested, should allow for appropriate modifications. For example, if access to transactions is being made from a travel application, perhaps additional actions such as (re)setting fraud indicators on financial transactions should be factored in. The better we anticipate potential actions, simplify the user interface, and trigger proactive customer notifications the more responsive the customer experience becomes. Understanding context also implies that we determine when something is not appropriate. Context should be built up and refined over time, and must span multiple industries that make up the connected customer journey.

Personalization

In the digital world, we are getting used to personalization. Personalization is not only good for marketing or sales, but also for efficient and effective service. Personalization is also a very potent method to achieve the purpose of helping customers manage their overall well-being such as financial, lifestyle and health. When we make decisions and take actions to help customers individually, that's called personalization. For example, updating and analyzing the customers' savings and spending goals to initiate a dialog. The possibilities are endless so I'd like to differentiate personalization from context by stating this: personalization is individual tailoring to open a dialog based on context and specific customer information. And as we discussed at the beginning of this chapter, we won't have data privacy issues if we personalize well. In fact, we have data privacy issues because we don't personalize and build context.

Augmenting the Primary Customer Relationship

There are many methods to provide these basic functions. In most cases, how the services are used will be controlled and orchestrated by the business that owns the customer experience at that moment of the customer journey. However, the way we design our model to engage and help a customer along their relationship is vital. In most cases, the business that owns the relationship may not want to provide services that are non-core to their business. That means that within the overall operating model, we have the option of:

1. Providing supplementary services to enhance the customer experience, and also maintain context and personalization data
2. Helping the front-end entity provide a seamless experience. Think of applying for credit from a retailer but then having to explicitly manage 2 different credit relationships – one with the retailer, and another with the bank that provided the loan.

White labeled products have been on offer for a while now so the business process implications of the ecosystem model are not new. For example, we have all been offered various warranty products on our retail purchases, or seen life insurance and co-branded cards being offered at big box retailers. In addition, almost all banks and credit card issuers offer retailer promotions and loans. These are all personalized to various degrees and are based on various types of direct integrations, or use of brokering platforms.

The battle for customer engagement in today's fast paced digital market has heated up. And the more seamless and contextual the integration is the better it is. Needless to say that the channels over which customers access our products has expanded significantly. Apart from traditional web and mobile access, customers are now expecting to see their favorite provider in places they frequent most. Opening up access through better integrations makes it easy for customers to embed us into transactions where they wouldn't think of us previously. It reduces friction in the commerce and fulfillment processes. For example, we can imagine looking up retailers in our online banking account for the right deals, and apply for a loan right there rather than having to fill out a credit application separately at the retailer.

In fact increased access and availability can allow us to act on our customers' behalf to help them make good choices. The biggest differentiator in the new world order will be how we can partner with our customers and look out for them. And that brings us to the next step in the roadmap.

Level 2: Originate Transactions & Own the Relationship

As industry boundaries collapse and explicit walls between various providers are destroyed, it is critically important to always be monitoring the place and value of our brand in our customers' minds. The impacts of not being able to do so can be disastrous. We recently saw agreements between Visa, MasterCard and PayPal to allow each other to be part of their ecosystems (see ref 21). With these agreements, PayPal got an entry into the networks' wallets for offline transactions, and the networks have made another attempt to maintain their position in PayPal's payment options list. It is obvious that much is at stake for all three players. More traditionally, many manufacturers today use platforms provided by Amazon and Walmart to advertise and sell their products. Using a 3rd party platform has its share of risks as we witnessed when Facebook changed its rules for business pages and network reach (see ref 22). Similarly, discovery on online retail platforms is a challenge. It's clear that every provider needs to think of how to get closer to their customers.

While news items like the Visa-MasterCard-PayPal deal are at a point in time, the underlying principles behind these news items are long lasting. Being an orchestrator of customer experience helps us avoid being relegated to being a behind-the-scenes service provider. There is nothing wrong with being a behind-the-scenes services provider too. But in both cases it is important to be scanning the market for potential disruptions and disintermediations, and to evolve our products and services accordingly. Especially, with technology offering up new capabilities at a blazingly fast speed, it takes less time today for something new to be adopted and become mainstream.

For this reason, it is worth revisiting the Customer Interaction Index. The index measures 2 dimensions of customer engagement:

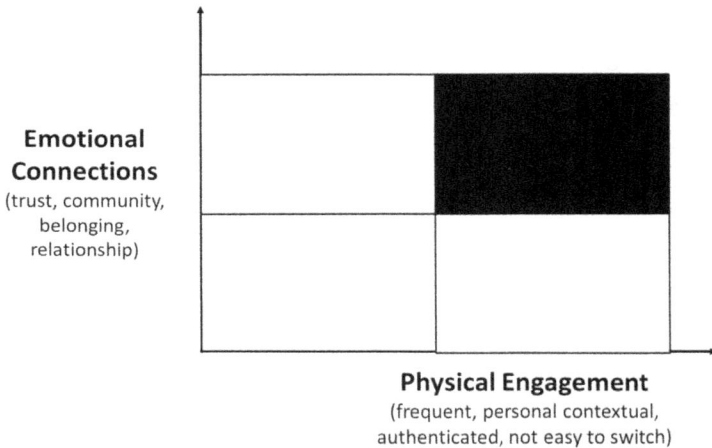

Emotional Connections
(trust, community, belonging, relationship)

Physical Engagement
(frequent, personal contextual, authenticated, not easy to switch)

Fig: The Customer Interaction Spectrum

Emotional

The strength of our brand is defined by the imprints we leave on our customers, the recall we can drive, and the emotional feelings that are triggered when our brand is mentioned. Individual brands are also affected positively or negatively by the brand of the industry as a whole. For example, almost all banks would trigger trust and security – sentiments that are associated with the industry as a whole. We are all aware of the legendary battles between Coke and Pepsi. This is also the reason we consider BMW an ultimate driving machine, and Volvo as the safest car for our families.

Physical or Fulfilment

The strength and frequency of our actual interaction with customers defines how many chances we get to be in front of our customers, and how sticky the relationship with customers is. Ranking high on this dimension implies that customers have gone through a process to sign up (investment), have a significant stake in the relationship (stickiness), and many of their daily actions have direct links to our business operations (interaction).

The index provides an easy way to understand which parts need to be strengthened to create a strong and sticky customer engagement.

- For example, most consumer retail brands and insurers would be on the top left, while banks will be on the top right. That's because traditionally brands have attempted to elevate the Emotional part of the engagement and in only a few cases been able to embed the brand promises into the physical part of the engagement.
- A payments or financial services firm is on the top right – strong on both emotional and physical fronts. Payments and banking is core to customers for many obvious reasons.

We can now devise strategies to bring these 2 ends of the spectrum together, and explore approaches to create new customer engagement models. For example new entrants into financial services are trying to break the strong bond that customers have with their banks. Some innovators have focused on creating their own place in the customer ecosystem by making spending management and lifestyle as the defining pivot. Emerging financial services companies are leveraging digital innovations to carve out a niche. For example, Divy, Clink and Acorns are helping customers save as they spend (see ref 23).

Hence, this second level of the roadmap is about taking the focus away from servicing transactions to being the originator of transactions. There are 2 forces which will help this transition. The first being that the barrage of digital capabilities being made available is also causing customers to be more skeptical of the value being offered. The evidence is obvious in the rise of the third-party-advice economy and the rise of content marketing. The second force is the fact that new and emerging players are breaking in to take on parts of the overall value proposition. This implies that the customer context itself is at the risk of being fragmented instead of being integrated. This second point gives hope to incumbents with broader service offerings. While seamless and intuitive experiences may drive quick adoption of new services, the power of context and trust cannot be underestimated.

For these reasons, the capabilities that need to be built should aim at consolidating customer context so that the targeting is much more individual and deterministic.

As you review these capabilities below, keep in mind that interactive tool kits such as the below are gaining renewed momentum. Before technology and digital opened up the market a few years ago, these capabilities were not widely developed because they could not muster up enough meat to satisfy the ROI (Return On Investment) considerations of the past. However in the new world, many such helpful digital capabilities can almost be considered costs of doing business, and keeping customers engaged. The speed of change in the market is so rapid that these incremental changes cannot be delayed or labeled as band aids if we are to reinforce our brands in the customers' minds. Constantly thinking about the business value of each incremental innovation contributes to that inertia. The business value instead should be recognized as a sum of these innovations.

- Generate demand through creation of wish lists that aim to create a fuller customer persona. Strategies to create wish lists can range from simply asking, to incremental accumulation of information through interactive digital tools such as future goal setting and assessments.
- Allow customers to create goals where transactions are linked to immediate and aspirational goals. Digital investments at enterprises have been heavily influenced in the past by the philosophy of predictive analytics and targeting. However, as we build our digital capabilities for the future, we should take advantage of the fact that customers are already beyond the critical trust threshold when it comes to sharing information. We have almost everything we need to help customers fulfilment their goals, whether they are about financial security, travel, or shopping.
- Allow tools for planning & short term gratification to be extended to customer networks. Traditionally we've kept individuals separate in our interactions. That obviously has very good reasons from a privacy standpoint. However, a

permission based capability that allows the goals, their planning, and money buckets to be linked as appropriate between customers as part of their social network – e.g. families, temporary purpose based groups - goes a long way towards understanding the dependencies and customers' decision making processes. In addition, it allows for short term goals to be met much more easily, and strengthens customer engagement. For example, leisure activities or short vacations can be worked towards in a collaborative way instead of separately.

- Build 2-way APIs with partners to ensure that customer engagement is both ways. While non-financial services companies such as Uber, United and Google are doing this already, financial services firms are still using centralized platforms for offer management and redemption. While such platforms help reduce complexity, they also only enable a 1-way dialog with retailers and other service providers. What's needed is a way for these other parties to be able to tap into each other to pull additional context of the transaction. This additional context can provide avenues for richer engagement, potentially cross-sell, and also enable them to abide by a customer's wish list or planning goals to build additional trust in the ecosystem.

The last statement of additional customer context now takes us to the 3rd level in the roadmap.

Level 3: Create Experiences & Connect Value

As I touched upon briefly in the description for level 2, additional digital capabilities today are also making customers more skeptical in the offers that are thrown to them. The onus of right decision making is being pushed to the customers, while each player in the system focuses on meeting its individual goals.

Some examples are:

1. Emergence of spend and save platforms that promise to pass along a small percentage of the transaction to a retirement or other investment account
2. Development of digital capabilities to deliver highly targeted non-banking retail promotions that are aimed at tapping into the customers inherent desire to purchase
3. Creation of interconnected services using Internet of Things (e.g. Amazon Alexa) that prompt and facilitate quick, single click (or voice command based) purchase and delivery

Payments and investments are disappearing behind a wall of convenience and highly interactive customer experience. However, although financial services firms have many of the same revenue and margin goals, they are also perhaps set to benefit significantly if they attempt to fulfil their role as custodians of their customers' overall financial well-being. With new regulations, and with tremendous public awareness around how financial services are changing, there is no doubt that banking, and to a large extent payments, are expected to look out for the customers, not just make money. The recent PSD2 directive (Payment Services Directive) in the UK, as well as the fiduciary and fee structure changes that were introduced in the US over the past several years are an outcome of the heated debate around this topic.

It turns out that those who can evolve their models quickly to become custodians of financial wellbeing will be the biggest beneficiaries. The model for the Customer Interaction Index outlined in the previous section serves as a reminder of the potential of the close customer relationships that already exist.

This final level in the roadmap will evaluate the capability of creating an ecosystem of cross-industry partnerships. Let's examine these from the perspective of financial services, and see how other industries such as retail and travel integrate with it. A new bank called Fidor in Germany has embarked on creating such an ecosystem already which can serve as an excellent reference baseline for how this capability needs to evolve (see ref 25).

- Being an orchestrator of services serving to enhance a customer's well-being is critical today. Such well-being can be measured through financial health, but has many other intangible aspects such as satisfaction with the activities being undertaken. Consider a customer who is buying camping gear for an adventure with friends. For firms across retail, travel, adventure, and banking, there is an open opportunity to help customers experience a complete picture of their obligations and needs. And incumbents arguably have an upper hand in this battle if they can leverage the trust, systems and customer portfolios they have built over the years. There are many digital technology innovations that can be leveraged for this purpose including warranties, advice and financial security. Similarly, robo-advising oriented tools (see ref 24) that can collaboratively build a picture of a customers' financial situation, and then recommend optimal actions are available today.

- Being an orchestrator outside of the financial industry is a logical and important step towards getting in front of the behind-the-scenes payments and banking trends. Various interfaces exist already in the form of card linked offers, co-branded cards and other mechanisms that have been developed over the years. What needs to be done is to move beyond the test and target models of today to more tailored and individual models of tomorrow. The interactive capabilities such as wish-lists built in the previous level of the roadmap will serve as a backbone of this orchestration.

- Developing a win-win with firms from multiple industries is needed to meet a customers end to end need. No single platform can or should try to capture a complete customer context. In fact it is impractical to do so. On the contrary, if various industry players work together along a published set of principles, they can help a customer make choices that satisfy fiduciary responsibilities. For example, retailers can query a wish-list or a money-bucket restriction before presenting a lucrative offer, and in turn provide certain transaction details to the bank so the customers profile can be kept updated. That's a much better model of building customer engagement and trust as against luring customers into deals they shouldn't be making. Sure enough, the human brain is wired to take risks and experience thrill, but there can be room for that as well in the new model.

Instead of being a service that satisfies requests in the back end, its best to create industry partnerships that allow you to develop smart accounts that maximize not only financial but overall well-being.

Skeptics will have many objections. For those who are skeptical of how this will work out given the inherent privacy and compliance risks, consider use of emerging technology paradigms such as blockchain (see ref 26). This distributed data model can be adapted such that no single entity can control the entire profile. In addition, customers can maintain their profiles and decide who to provide permissions to. All said and done, customer permissions and privacy are an important requirement of any ecosystem we are part of. Skeptics may also be worried about sales impacts if they have to think of the customer wellbeing at every stage. Suffice it to say that the quality of customers we acquire, and how we acquire them have important ramifications for most businesses on the total customer value front (see ref 27).

Managing Commoditization Versus Complexity

Connecting to platforms often leads to commoditization that is mitigated only by the sheer volume of the data and customers that the platform services. However no single platform can truly serve the personalized needs of customers and their uniquely diverse nature of profiles. Even Facebook and Amazon have to resort to predictive analytics and continuous guesswork to bombard customers with redundant offers and advertisements.

However, decreasing the level of commoditization often requires a corresponding increase in complexity of interactions. The complexity increases because the platforms must interact with and orchestrate the customer profile through many different connected platforms. For example, Amazon as a retailer probably has little insight into the usage behavior after a product is sold. The introduction of Amazon Echo is an attempt to get into the middle of that interaction. Similarly, credit card issuers lack line-item level transaction data. And Citi's Price Rewind program is probably a way to build that context while providing an invaluable service to customers. In a distributed and connected network of platforms, the concept of simple targeting will give way to more intuitive – perhaps deep learning based – algorithms that will serve their customer masters, instead of the platform creators.

Primary Challenges With Implementation

In a digital, connected world, the first biggest challenge is to be able to understand and envision the way we want to play in this rapidly changing market. While traditional revenue models will be difficult to change rapidly, the key to success will be in embracing new ways of bringing together the various parties that make up the value chain your business operates in. What this means is that any product or service customers buy from you is surrounded by products and services that your firm may not be dealing with today.

As products and services become increasingly commoditized and similar in basic characteristics, the difference in customer experience will be in meeting needs that are influencers. For example, a bank provides checking accounts, but the balances that customers keep at the bank depend on their savings patterns, investment priorities and their spending patterns. How well does a bank bring these influencing factors together will probably be the defining factor is how their strategy evolves.

Not only does such a vision drive customer and account growth as in the above banking example, thinking about influencing factors also affect profitability. For example, when health insurers partner with fitness providers, not only do they build stickiness into their products, but they also are able to influence their claims ratios. Further, the additional insights they gather on their customers helps them improve their underwriting processes.

In short, the big difference in today's connected world is that an ecosystem needs to be built around core products and services. It's easier today than ever before due to much better API management, availability of cloud platforms, abundance of better analytics tools, and the ubiquity of mobile, among other developments.

The concept of channels takes on a new meaning too. In the past channels were the ways we reached customers on our own and made them easier to transact with us. So we tried to be available on mobile, web, social media etc. The intent was that customers should be able to access us anywhere, anytime. In a connected world, we will now need to think about common customers. For example, Uber is striking partnerships with other providers such as United airlines who own their part of the customer experience. When customers look up the United app for their flight time, Uber is right there for them to get to the airport.

In the future, as customer interaction moves to chatbots and voice activated front ends, it is important to consider these additional means of customer engagement and build integrations to address them. Everything cannot be left up to the customer to initiate. And fortunately, technology allows us today to sign up customers for implicit transactions. If I'm speaking to the United chatbot to check me in, can the bot also invoke Uber and book a ride for me. These types of integrations are neither absolutely new nor too far away in the future to be available more commonly. But the term "channels" is taking on new meanings. You can be standing in your kitchen asking Apple Siri to check you in, and Siri may ask you if you need a cab.

The third big consideration is about customer reach and engagement. Being available where customers are is great, but how do you get them to prioritize you over other providers. Common marketing tactics such as promotions, loyalty programs, discounts and advertisements are excellent tools to create that initial engagement and trial use. However, as choice of service providers increases, it is important again to go back to the concept of an ecosystem.

For example, in our travel scenario above, what if the customer uses both Lyft and Uber? How does Siri or United make the decision for the customer? What makes the customer choose one over the other? The difference will be in bringing the influencing needs of customers into the equation. In our travel scenario, hotels and Airbnb may be a logical extension, or perhaps tour operators can be brought into the mix to create just the right incentive for customers to choose your service over the other.

This same concept can be extended to financial services and payments as well. What payment method I use today depends on my core product characteristics such as cash back or airline miles. What if the credit card links my short term goals such as upcoming travel budget, and ties it together with the retailer. Together the two parties can trump the card instrument that has perhaps higher cash back or airlines miles per transaction.

Summary

The promise of the future is that the world will be connected. But it won't be just about developing platforms. In fact the platforms we are building today will be inadequate to drive customer engagement and commerce of the future.

Why is that? That's simply because our customers are human and connected. In fact, the focused and specific platforms of today will become components of much larger platforms. These larger interconnected platforms will logically arise as a result of collaboration between innovators and their individual platforms. They will connect with each other to complement their own capabilities, and probably also try to compete with one another. The big difference will be in how the logical platforms allow creation of context and value. As the world changes, we need to create a place in the new order of our customers' minds.

I touched upon 5 principles that will allow creation of interconnected platforms in my book *Dancing The Digital Tune*. This book outlines in more detail the frameworks and methodology that will allow you to create interconnected platforms. These platforms in turn will create the high levels of customer engagement and intimacy that is needed for the connected world.

However, one thought keeps coming up: Is the first step of this journey really the wholesale core technology and delivery transformation? Should that take place before we can do anything else? In my opinion, upgrade of technology is a reality that must be met as soon as possible. Doing so will help us deliver more efficiently. However, the immediate challenges have to do with customer engagement, differentiation, and building of context.

For example, if we look at what's happening in the banking sector, it is actually the higher purpose of financial money management and financial well-being through which the sector is being disrupted. Innovations are cropping up and aiming to meet peripheral customer needs. Such innovations include personal financial management, saving for retirement and education, peer to peer payment transactions, lifestyle needs, product warranties, lending and mortgages, broad based loyalty management, and so on. As a result, it is evident that simply supplying various (and disjointed) products and services to customers to choose is not proving to be enough. We need to actively help customers with their goals.

Therefore the connected roadmap in this chapter should be thought of as a Rubik's cube of capabilities. As digital innovations drive customer experience based engagement, the underlying core is becoming more and more invisible and undifferentiated. Given this trend, step 2 of the model to build context assumes higher importance. Although innovations in individual product lines provide better and effortless customer experience, the silo transactions may actually be causing defragmentation of customer engagement. So we should be looking at integrating the customer context where possible to drive immediate impact. Here step 3 of the model to build partnerships takes priority. Those who have scale can start with Step 1 to build strong momentum in a broader market. But for others, there's actually an opportunity to solve for customer engagement and context first. The underlying enabler will still be technology but they can first focus on creating models of customer and community engagement. These models will then demand various building blocks. And based on these we can then properly utilize and structure the core, if at all we can call it that in the future.

BLOCK 1: ECOSYSTEM BASED CX

One of the primary goals of the "Connected Company" framework is customer engagement. The term customer engagement, as also customer experience takes on a new meaning in the connected context. In this chapter let's discuss the need to focus on Ecosystem based CX instead of company specific CX.

Traditionally, we've relied on industry based customer personas and use cases. But as we move towards a connected world, these use cases and personas will be woefully inadequate. The value we bring to our clients may look to be exceptional if we look inwardly, but to the customer, we appear to be stuck in the stone-age.

Consider these examples:

- The financial technology (FinTech) revolution is emerging in the banking industry. Banks have excellent products and robust risk management procedures. They even have free checking accounts, great cash back programs and even protect us 100% in case of fraud on our cards and accounts. But they are far from being the heroes today. Instead our heroes are those that are able to capture the customer front end, look beyond the core banking products and provide a service which banks fail to do. Our hero is the mobile phone app that takes the change from our retail spend and invests it into a retirement account. Or the app that lives off commissions on payments transactions but provides a seamless experience (see ref 23).

- Retailers are trying to reach customers by way of coupons, promotions and deals of the week. We've reached a point where customers have become so accustomed to price discounts that a deal must always be present, and customers will always double check it too! Efforts to change this model have resulted in huge failures, most notably and recently at J.C. Penney (see ref 28). Moreover, an offer never reaches customers when they need it. To the customers, despite all our attractive stores and technology, we are still stuck with the marketing models of the old. If customers are actively engaged the game can be instantly raised by many levels. Many retailers are also partnering with the mobile apps of our banks to provide us with deals (e.g. card linked offers). This capability helps both retailers and banks create new ecosystems around the customer and raise the level of one-one dialog and wish-lists. The difference this approach brings from bulk campaigns is profound – especially because we combine a sticky relationship (banking) with a fleeting relationship (retail). Such an approach also mitigates the privacy conundrum plaguing the industries. The Customer Interaction Spectrum introduced earlier explains this well and is an integral part of the Ecosystem Based CX framework.

It is clear that Ecosystem based CX is the need of the future. Consider the following additional scenarios where industry boundaries can be transcended:

1. A retailer partnering with a fitness center to better personalize both sides of the customer experience and commerce

2. A travel agency partnering with a bank to manage 3rd party local payments and risk management. Both of these examples will leverage digital ecosystems to deliver the experience.

3. A bank partnering with retailers and brand organizations to push personalized promotions to their customers.

As is evident, industry based personas and use cases have their places to plan and execute business processes such as support and sales. But they are grossly insufficient to drive the customer experience of the future. We need to build real customer personas, which by their very definition cannot be limited to an industry alone. We need to think of our customers as people. But the customer engagement journey has been slow despite several recent technological advances. The techniques and how to use them have become the strategy, and the bigger picture has been lost. There are 2 reasons for that.

First, there's been a lot of debate about the difference between customer experience and customer engagement. For the purposes of this book I will take the position that customer experience is only one of the many factors that drives customer engagement. That's because a lot of intangible aspects such as price, differentiation, emotional branding, the ability to secure trust, and so many other factors define how customers will engage with us. As we will see throughout the rest of this book, customer experience itself is defined by a myriad of mechanisms. Customer experience is fleeting and lacking at times (e.g. response to a high price or a sub-optimal customer service experience). However it is how we react, and then how the customer responds that defines customer engagement. Are we able to engage and keep customers engaged with us so that we maintain the position of trust in their minds despite occasional hiccups? If yes, then this approach is what ultimately defines customer engagement.

Second, the traditional definition of customer engagement has been characterized by the touch-points we end up converting with respect to an action. Whether it is more time spent on the website, responding to a promotional offer, opening our email, or several such metrics, these are all important and depict how customers respond to us. But they have also rendered customer engagement to be very transactional. Consider any industry that is characterized by a low Customer Interaction Index.

Industries with a low Customer Interaction Index are typically those that do not have a strong underlying relationship – whose collective score on both the emotional and physical dimensions is low. For example retail brands and consumer packaged goods will fall under this category. The focus on transactional metrics in such industries is in stark evidence as despite significant advances in technology, much of this industry hasn't been able to move past mass promotional campaigns across all channels.

We should ask ourselves about the last time we received a promotional email that offered us something that was requested and agreed upon, as against a promotion that was inferenced based on our actions. The use of advanced analytics to guess what customers want comes naturally to these industries because they are unable to establish a sticky relationship with customers, despite them having a strong emotional connection.

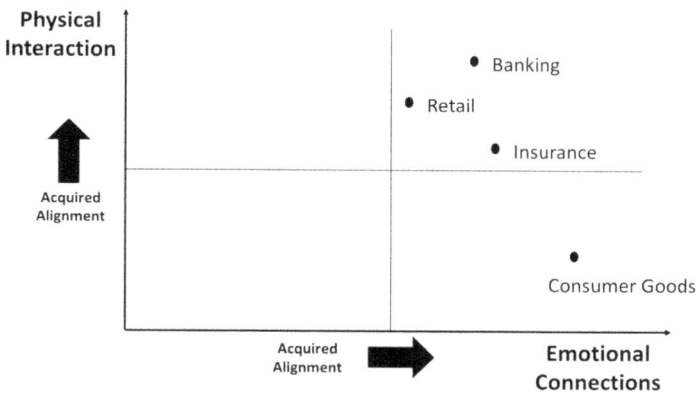

Fig: Representative Natural Customer Interaction Index of Some Common Industries

The next diagram indicates the engagement chasm that arises out of this technologically advanced but primitive approach. This is also where most privacy and personalization issues arise because we do not have customer consent or buy-in to engage with them.

We've been asking and thirsting for relevant offers, but all we get thrown at us is the result of advanced analytics done at the mass level. The industry has been guessing, and the guessing game has just got a little better, but they haven't yet begun to engage with us. The industry hasn't been able to understand the customer personas and is only trying to insert itself into relevant and timely conversations.

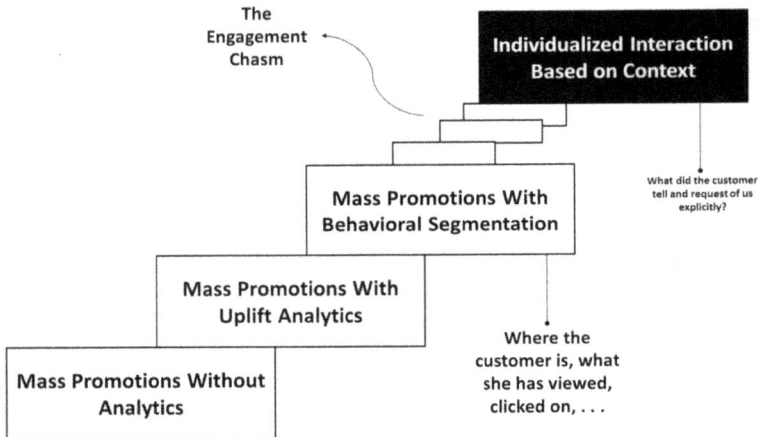

The Engagement Chasm

Individualized Interaction Based on Context

What did the customer tell and request of us explicitly?

Mass Promotions With Behavioral Segmentation

Mass Promotions With Uplift Analytics

Mass Promotions Without Analytics

Where the customer is, what she has viewed, clicked on, . . .

Fig: The Chasm of Customer Engagement

On the one hand a commonly reason cited for lack of personalization is concern for customer privacy. On the other hand we are witness to an entire banking revolution where exactly this high level of interactivity is causing a massive turmoil in an established and heavily regulated industry. Industries such as banking and insurance that enjoy constant access to the customers by virtue of accounts, have absolutely been struggling to build on the strong and intimate relationships they enjoy with customers. Where they should be engaging customers into a detailed persona building exercise, we see absolute lack of coordination between channels, and impersonal, uneducated sales processes. No wonder that banks are seen as undifferentiated by customers (see ref 29). Legacy technology and regulations are cited as common reasons, but instead it is the failure to drive customer engagement in a connected world.

To address and resolve this dismal state of affairs, the framework we are examining intends to achieve customer engagement in a deliberate, systematic manner. The capabilities that support this goal are comprehensive and should form the core of the CEOs agenda. They should be driven by a leadership that recognizes that to survive in today's connected world, customer engagement must be driven from the top down. Operational and silo metrics such as customer service friendliness will not suffice.

Now let's see how to create the first capability in our framework that will propel us into the future. This capability is about creating Ecosystem based CX:

- **Extend the personas:** Before we can create ecosystem based CX, we need to define the right personas. Traditional customer personas and segment information will not be adequate so we must extend them. Most of us already have these traditional personas built out.
- **Develop connected customer journeys**: Begin to create and fulfil the customer journeys across our partner network through cross-industry engagement.

Extend the Personas

One of the most commonly cited issues by businesses is that they don't know their customers as well as they should. The underlying problem is not the lack of pretty documents called customer personas with a nice pseudo name and photograph. Instead the issue is that the customer personas are not effective enough.

We are all used to creating customer personas. These are useful tools to understand and segment customers so we can take useful action to serve them. A useful metric we often refer to is the lifetime value. We develop personas because the more personalized and granular we get, the more we can reduce our operational costs (e.g. how we handle phone calls or returns), and the better we can maximize our revenue (e.g. buy more, buy frequently, up sell, cross sell, get referrals etc.). Personas are most known to be used by marketing because they are most vocal about it. But almost every function and department leverages personas even though they may not be creating pretty documents on them.

We often base personas on both quantitative and qualitative data by looking at demographics, behaviors, beliefs, etc. For example, a technology software company may segment its audience by industry, then role, then function, e.g. VP of customer analytics in a consumer packaged goods firm. And then develop personas based on what they know about this type of person so it is easier to reach them, and connect with them. A VP in a large company may respond differently, and so might a person who has an efficiency focus versus an innovation focus, and so on.

Traditionally personas have been all about us and our customers. We look at who our customers are, what purpose they are trying to fulfil, what are their motivations, how they make their buying (or other) decisions, how they buy (or interact), and other such questions. Then we try to define our programs around them.

The problem with the traditional approach is that it is not suited very well for a connected world. In an age when digital technology is making it easier for customers to interact seamlessly across industry boundaries, how can we develop a persona, and then act on it in isolation?

There are two major problems with the traditional approach:

1. The personas are not complete
2. Our plan to address the personas is impeded by our thought process.

The reason I say that the personas are not complete is because they are not made with the ecosystem in mind. Hence they don't provide actionable insights into things that don't concern our product directly. For example, imagine we own a retail store (or bank, or a car dealership, etc.). We might understand that persona A comes to our store when they have an event coming up. So our marketing outreach will attempt to analyze and reach out to people who fit the criteria, and our sales process ay identify a certain set of activities or products to stock. This outreach is strenuous and does not lend itself to effective personalization. The persona is incomplete because it misses out on valuable information including motivations for attending the event. It also missed out the needs of the persona that are not directly about our products.

In addition to incomplete personas, this example also highlights how we act in a limited fashion because our thought process is constrained by the artificial boundaries we set for ourselves. Our customers may be members of an association, or belong to a community, have strong social beliefs, or may have professional reasons, and so on. The company that manages the events or membership to those associations that are linked to the events will have much better emotional and physical connections with these customers. They will also have much more data than a retail store can reasonably gather. Hence if a network of companies comes together to sign a contract (a logical contract) with the customers to serve them better, it's a win-win for all. This is not just a channel or distribution partnership. Instead it's a partnership to engage customers better with mutual benefits. The store can provide reliable service, perhaps a discount, and the event can hope to improve retention rates, and even possibly get new customers who may not already be in its audience. The customers are better assured of their privacy, and get a better value overall. This is easy to come by through cross-company collaboration, and by taking the customer into confidence based on their (more) complete personas. Customer privacy issues are automatically addressed as well.

To make the example above work, customer journeys must work both ways:

1. How do we handle customer journeys specific to our own business?
2. How do we meet the aspirations of our partners?

Our traditional personas handle the first problem. But hardly any of us think of the second problem. In a connected world, the second problem is critical to solve if we are to reap the real benefits of the ecosystems that are being formed.

How exactly should we establish these partnerships between companies? I cover that in the chapter on Integration where we will discuss how to identify the right partners, how to align priorities and how to go about creating an ecosystem. For the purposes of this chapter, let's come up with a model for customer personas we should strive for.

A Sample Customer Persona

Let's consider a B2B persona for a change. Imagine we are a software product company that makes email marketing software. One of the key trends this company hears about is that technology spending is moving from the Chief Information Officer to the Chief Marketing Officer. Using this trend, they decide to focus on the marketing managers who they suspect will have the budgets, as well as will have the decision making authority. Let's consider the persona of a marketing manager who will be a key buyer (with the blessings of the CMO and CFO of course).

A typical person includes the following:

1. **A nice persona name**: Let's call this marketing manager Karen
2. **Demographics, Education:** mid-twenties to late thirties, mostly women but some men, generally a bachelors or MBA degree in marketing, arts, communications. These days having some technology and social media campaign management experience is common

3. **Responsibilities:** All the nice stuff about working with the business, strategizing, aligning goals, developing plans, making customer personas, writing email copy, tracking results, sending to CRM, maximizing conversions, generating reports, working well in a team etc.

4. **Sources of information:** Generally a list of common items such as professionals and peers, some known websites, some famous conferences, social media (of course) etc.

5. **Current pain areas:** Generally a repetition of our sales or marketing pitch – strapped for time, needs to focus on business outcomes, needs more reports and analytics, always in search of the right talent, no one fully understands the value of what Karen does etc.

6. **Success factors expected from our solution:** Generally a rehash of our own marketing and sales pitch – easy, flexible, scalable, full control, lots of features, all information on fingertips, cost not a factor if value provided etc. Single view of customer is a common item included here.

7. **Barriers to decision making:** Again a rehash of commonly known industry wide limitations like trust in our company viability and product roadmap, email deliverability concerns, wish-list items that mirror MS Outlook and those that no one provides yet etc.

8. **What the buying journey looks like:** Again a common set of items that are so common you'd think they'll be different in a highly confidential persona – need to see a demo, need competitive benchmarking, need testimonials, case studies, need support during adoption etc.

A lot of the insights that go into the persona come from quantitative data sources like surveys, first hand observations, analytics of past sales and marketing data, web analytics, 3rd party research etc.

This persona is actually great! But in my view it is somewhat inadequate. What are the additional items that we might include?

1. **Pain areas beyond our product:** When Karen is not sending email what is she spending her time on? E.g. getting the right content to link to in an email, making a high quality database, following through on the leads to ensure sales gives her credit, taking stock of other marketing activities that result in or result from emails, ensuring the landing pages are done right by the web team, struggling with CRM configuration issues, and so on

2. **Partners who complement my software:** Does Karen work with content agencies, which CRM does her company use, who helps with the CRM, where does her database come from, how does she maintain it?

3. **Partners who help Karen's stakeholders:** Karen's prime stakeholders are the business teams within her own company. What do they sell and how are they differentiating themselves, do they use partners or suppliers to make or sell the core product?

4. **Partners who help Karen's customers:** We are getting way beyond Karen's job description now but this is the business strategy she is actually supporting with the software. Who's buying the company's products and what are their needs and pain points. How do you understand and reach them most effectively? By helping her with this question, you help Karen (and her boss) become better partners to their business. And this opens the doors to bigger conversations.

Budgets for email marketing software don't seem a big constraint now.

The real challenges with any buying process are not the feature set of the product being sold. It's all the other things that influence the decisions, which in turn affect the budgets available. If Karen's boss (the CMO) has to spend her money on all these other items, then a snappy email software with lots of great features that grows with the company's needs, becomes a lower priority. They need to fix the content first, they must get the CRM up and running much better, and they need to define the core business value propositions better. All those things take priority.

As a supplier of email marketing software, these are all items that should go into our sales kit. And we don't need to build all these capabilities ourselves. We just need to know our customers better so we can plan out who we should partner with, or leverage, to address these aspects. It could be as simple as sharing a research report on Karen's customers that she can share with her stakeholders, and providing advice on how to best get her CRM configured. There are other providers who would much appreciate introductions for brief consulting workshops because they'd like to sell to Karen's company too. And they would reciprocate for sure. So we get a win both ways.

By considering these extended aspects of our traditional customer personas, we start thinking of the principles of partnerships and ecosystem building. We build multiple entry points into our customers' buying journey. Weren't these principles that actually gave rise to the field of content marketing? However, we sometimes forget to walk the talk. We get so engrossed in meeting our tactical goals, that we lose sight of the principles. We talk about collaboration but then forget to cultivate and collaborate with important partners. We sell, but we don't build a selling machine. As a buyer, I myself have been approached by many companies, and I can testify that those that won my business were those that met my apparently peripheral needs head on.

Develop Connected Customer Journeys

Now that we have the extended customer personas, how do we build appropriate customer journeys? A customer journey is an outlining of the touch-points, mediums of interactions, and the tools we use to engage the customer across these touchpoints.

A few years ago, we started on the path of multichannel customer journeys which aligned our messaging and approach across various channels such as phone, web, email and in-person. The multichannel approach was an inside-out strategy but it was much needed to improve the quality of customer engagement. If we aren't consistent in our messaging and approach across channels, would customers feel comfortable? Would we be effective in communicating our value propositions? There is no doubt that the multichannel approach was a major step forward. Technological enhancements such as shared databases, and quality content management made it easier to adopt such as approach.

From multichannel we then moved to an Omni Channel approach. The subtle difference being that the new approach looked at customer journeys from an outside-in perspective. What should the client journey look like and how can we remove the breaks in customer experience? Customers move across channels and touch-points, and the experiences have to relate to their latest interactions and status on various channels. A customer calling into our contact center should be spoken to in a different way if they have recently interacted on our website, or visited us in-person. This notion of Omni Channel has still not been fully realized but there is tremendous progress being made. It is obvious how improvements on this front can lead to tangible and immediate increases in customer acquisition and retention rates.

However, the concept of Omni Channel needs a facelift when we consider a digital, connected marketplace. It needs to consider cross-industry interactions. The world is also moving faster than it was a few years ago. Innovations in technology are making it easier for nimble companies to address these problems faster than their larger and slower competitors. In addition, the business domains are being better understood causing talent to move on across companies with ideas they find easier to implement at nimble firms. The advances by technology companies such as Amazon, Facebook, PayPal among others are using this talent to create a larger impact.

That said, the world always moves faster than what current capabilities can offer. And that is the reason there is always opportunity to catch up, and even leapfrog the early movers. Just when brick and mortar firms were catching up with the online business challenges, their physical assets became more important than ever in meeting the ever increasing expectations of immediate fulfilment. And now innovations in drone delivery and shared economy are opening up the supply, distribution and fulfillment sides of the business. There is a large indirect workforce available who will gladly distribute and even acquire customers on our behalf to scale up their own business models. Who will tap into this ecosystem first? And can they sustain their innovation head start?

All of this makes the connected customer journey more important than ever. A connected customer journey understands and leverages the customer interactions of other players in the industry, and most definitely of players from other industries. For example, a retailer will leverage not only distribution partners, but perhaps also partner with travel and entertainment companies. One of the biggest issues with traditional business that the connected world changes dramatically is the notion of customer insight. Deriving predictive insights from mountains of data to improve the guesswork of what the customer will do next is becoming the old model. The new model is about striking up a dialog so you "know" what the customer wants from you, and has agreed for you to deliver it. This is what a connected customer journey helps you achieve.

A Sample Customer Journey

Customer journey mapping has become a very useful tool over the past decade as multichannel and Omni Channel models started to become easier through technology. Traditional customer journey mapping essentially considers the following:

1. **Channels over which customers interact:** These are typically websites, mobile sites or apps, social media platforms such as Facebook or LinkedIn, phone or contact center, stores or physical mediums, physical mail, etc. The philosophy is that if customers have to interact with us, they

use one or more of these channels to research, buy and get customer service.

2. **The primary perceived utility of the channels:** Each of the above channels is associated with what the customers use it for. For example, customers may begin their journey on a search engine like Google, move over to do additional research over your websites, continue on mobile, and finally end up in the store or branch.

However, there are 4 additional aspects that must be included in traditional journeys:

1. **Iterative nature of the journey**: In most cases, the path to purchase is never a straight and sequential process. Customers need time to convince themselves of their underlying need, have offline conversations, look at testimonials, compare products from multiple providers, and so on. It is likely that they end up on our channels with different utility in mind than the ones we made our customer journey with. For example, a first time user on our website may be looking to see if we have products of a particular type available. And if customers visit for a second time, they may actually be looking for specific information on features, pricing or quality. Technology allows us today to monitor these repeat visits and offer up tailored experiences depending on these visits. It's easier for us to direct customers to different actions depending on what they have already done before.

2. **External reinforcement needed:** Almost every customer needs reinforcement or convincing on product quality and utility. There are 2 kinds of reinforcement. The first one is about providing proof points for our own products, and

tools to accomplish this are well known. For example, we make available customer reviews, third party seals of approval, case studies or testimonials from customers etc. However, the second type of reinforcement is perhaps more important than ever and which we don't usually think of. This is about ensuring that we embed ourselves into our customer's decision cycle. One of the most common breaks in customer journeys is when a customer goes to a third party or to your competitors in order to compare different products. Instead, by becoming a trusted source of this information, we can retain customers within our sphere of influence. As I outlined in *Dancing The Digital Tune*, acquiring the right customers is as important as just acquiring customers. So, external reinforcement speeds up the decision cycle, results in self-selection by customers, and improves the overall lifetime value of the customers for you. For example, in a study by Journal of Marketing Research of the American Marketing Associations (see ref 10), it was shown that promotional discounts based acquisitions result in lower repurchase levels. While every business and promotional strategy is different, this is an important principle to remember as we define and tailor our customer journeys. Acquiring the right customers is critical, and we can only hope to do that, if we are not afraid to provide external reinforcement.

3. **Interactive elements to reinforce connections**: We often talk about creating a relationship with customers. But the real challenge is how we need to achieve this. How do we match our platonic or emotional claims such as trust and high quality with actual physical engagement points which customers can experience? In *Dancing The Digital Tune*, I

outlined *The Principle of Customer Interaction*, which showed how important it is to connect the physical and emotional aspects of our brand. One of the easiest ways to do this in the digital world is to build interactive tools that help customers assess their own need and how a product fits in. These interactive tools then become entry points into a unique dialog that competitors can find hard to match. Various studies including one by MIT Sloan called "Is Customer Advocacy for you?" (see ref 12) shows that once your brand or company becomes a reference point in customers' minds, they keep coming back to you to finalize their product selection, offering you opportunities to make them a paid and loyal customer. In summary, trust and brand consideration go hand in hand.

4. **External players in the ecosystem:** Now we come to the most important element that is also the central theme of this book. How do we build an ecosystem for our customers? This is the most overlooked aspect of the customer journeys we develop and analyze. Our customer journeys are focused only on ourselves as if we are the center of the customer's universe. I have some bad news. We are not the center of their universe. In fact, every individual feels that they are at the center of the universe, and expects us to organize as per that notion (see ref 30). When it comes to customer journey mapping, we conveniently forget that customers are doing a million activities in addition to interacting with us. And a lot of those activities are indirectly linked to us. So our customer journey mapping should take those interactions into account.

For example, we conveniently include that customer do research on our website. But we forget what drove them there, and how can we build engagement on that channel. Our starting point for future strategy erroneously becomes the website, when in fact it should be the partner (and I don't mean channel) that drove the customers to our website. What were customers doing when they clicked through? That questions opens up an entire world of interactions that don't even factor in our customer journey. In fact, that's probably the one reason that customer journeys are decorative artifacts limited to web marketing or digital advertising, and not very useful for overall marketing strategy.

A simple example of this is a retailer that sells health food. We know that most customers who buy health foods probably already have or are thinking of engaging in various fitness activities. Structuring our program to include those 3rd parties that are actually the real owners of customer fitness should be top of our agenda. We can build out similar scenarios for banking and insurance as well. Instead, we think that the customer journey starts when they visit the store or when they browse our websites, or search for our products on their mobile phones while sitting in the train.

Here's are some wonderful examples of how this whole concept is being executed.

- Lifetime Fitness and Horizon Blue Cross Blue Shield of Jersey have partnered to link fitness with health insurance. Customers gain discounts if they focus on fitness. It's an excellent two-way relationship where both parties benefit tremendously.

- Uber, the famous online taxi company if I may call them, is helping drivers open bank accounts and retirement accounts with a new financial services company called Betterment. Most traditional drivers don't have a strong background in financial planning because of the way banking has been for several decades (the technical term for the issue is financial inclusion). And as Uber branches out broader into the travel sector, this is a great way in which both companies can help their customers meet their financial goals, as well as meet each other's needs as well.

- Through Apple Pay, smart financial services companies are finding ways to leverage the customer momentum rather than fight it. For example, companies like Capital One are now developing loyalty programs that tightly integrate with Apple Pay. Both companies win.

Summary

Underlying our discussion on customer persona development and customer journey mapping is the idea of the overall purpose of the customers. We cannot build effective customer journeys or personas without putting ourselves at the center of the customer's universe. This chapter brought our several important factors to consider as we build our customer personas and journeys.

We must think beyond our products portfolio to begin to understand the customers overall purpose and need. This analysis is no doubt at the heart of everything we do, but it needs to start becoming front and center of our customer engagement efforts. Because, the more we make it visible, the more our business processes will adapt to imbibe these principles. Its complex as it is to operate in functional silos because we all have goals to meet and tangible results to deliver. Positioning the overall purpose of our customers as a focal point for all channels and interactions makes it easier to collaborate across functions. Various functions and products can then come together to be competitors to maximize value, rather than acting as opponents and minimizing overall customer value.

Second and equally important is that we should build connected customer journeys. Customer journeys don't start with us. We are part of a bigger process. We should acknowledge that and begin to create connections outside our companies. We already do that effectively when it comes to marketing partners, distribution partners or service partners. We reach out and partner with other companies to provide warranty services, field services, and often installation services. But we need to start reaching out across industries to address the entire journey. One way is to acquire and become a bigger company as Amazon, Salesforce, Adobe, Walmart, and Google are doing. The other approach is to partner with other companies to create effective customer journeys. We saw that in the way Lifetime Fitness is partnering with Horizon health insurance.

We'll cover several techniques as we go along on loyalty, customer engagement, ecosystem building and of course how to gear up organizationally to manage the execution. But if you are taking a break from reading, spend some time to evaluate and think about your customer personas and customer journeys.

BLOCK 2: 3-TIER MODEL OF CUSTOMER LOYALTY

Loyalty programs are everywhere. According to a study by COLLOQUY (see ref 4), the average household in the US has over 29 loyalty program memberships but actively uses only 44% of these. The study also pointed out that 58% of customers don't even bother to participate and are less engaged members.

Customer engagement and loyalty are 2 very closely linked topics. Every business needs loyal customers. We need customers to buy from us rather than our competition. Promotions and discounts are universally followed to secure this attention and loyalty – incentivizing customers to buy from us by way of cash value rather than creating any long term differentiation. Sometimes, and much more effective, these offers are a means to get customers to try out or test the long term differentiation claimed.

Nothing is perfect, and while loyalty programs are a must to support our marketing and sales efforts, we must ask if the focus is too strongly tilted towards earning rewards that translate into discounts in return.

- Could these programs just be training customers to expect more for less?
- How are these programs yielding long term results by way of brand kinship?
- And finally the cause and effect paradox: were loyalty program users already more engaged to start with?

In this chapter let's do a deep dive into some of the broader aspects of customer engagement and loyalty, and how the model for a *Connected!* world may look like. In addition to bringing out important evolutions to the core loyalty program concept, I'll also outline how the loyalty programs must change to straddle industry boundaries.

First, let's review a very quick primer on the economics (financial and business case aspects) of loyalty so we can understand the nuts and bolts. A lot of our discussion in this chapter will be to influence these various levers that influence customer relationships and financial results.

A Very Rapid Primer on Loyalty Economics

The simplest way to understand the basics of traditional loyalty programs is this.

- What additional money are we spending?
- What additional returns are we receiving?

The additional money we spend on customers is all the points, perks, or cash discounts we give them in exchange for transacting with us:

- Cash back or points for transactions
- Giving them access to a dedicated account manager
- Providing quicker service
- Creating special websites for a particular segment
- Giving them discounts on other services that we don't provide (e.g. a Costco member gets discounts for car insurance, home improvement services etc.)
- And so on.

The additional benefits we get can be either immediate or long term:

- Additional volume of transactions by customers (more customers, more often)
- Larger transactions by customers (buying more at the same time)
- Customers sticking to us longer (retention rates)
- Easy to get new customers (acquisition rates and costs)
- Less price sensitivity because they trust us to deliver better overall value
- And so on.

In summary, we call this concept as increasing the Customer Lifetime Value – the net that remains after we take all gains over a long period of time, and subtract all the additional money we spend to make that happen. Some of it is easy to calculate, and a lot of it is difficult.

In addition, the core loyalty program has a concept called as redemption cost of reward points. This just depicts the actual cash value of the benefits we are returning to the customers. A 1% cashback program is straightforward. But giving customers 1 mile per dollar spent is a little less intuitive. While customers have come to broadly expect about 1% return on their spending, airlines can resort to various tactics to reduce their costs by running promotions during less popular times to less popular destinations. Or exactly the reverse!

We must also include the concept of financial liability. Every loyalty point given to customers is a promise to give them something in return later. And that implies that the company is accepting a future liability on their balance sheet. All these points have to be paid back. Companies often manage this liability by providing frequent redemptions to customers, or by setting an expiry on the points. Loyalty redemption – or exchanging points for goods or services – is an expense and also a liability. But if redemptions happen early and more frequently, they drive earnings which generate a positive cycle of customer engagement and more opportunities. Redemptions may also serve as reinforcement for pursuing long term goals (aspirational).

That's the end of this short primer. Broadly, keep in mind the following items as you read on:

1. Customer Lifetime value – are more customers spending more, more often
2. Redemption costs – what do the rewards cost us
3. Liability – Can we survive if all customers redeem everything at once

If we look deep into the loyalty economics model, the mathematics can get complex. Not only do we have to think about how much we are spending to give out rewards, but we must also think about how much future liability we are building up for rewards that we are not paying out.

As you read about the 3-tier model of loyalty, think of how it will help us balance these priorities through traditional techniques which can be implemented in a different way using the model.

Balancing the Operational and Strategic Perspectives

Any executioner knows that a strategic program has 2 simultaneous imperatives. We must continue to deliver results even while planning to build an engine that can fuel differentiation and results in the future. These two balancing perspectives apply to loyalty as well. How do we keep customers coming in, and at the same time plan a model that capitalizes on industry and technological trends. Both of these perspectives are important in their own right. It is exactly for this reason that strategic change is difficult. This type of change requires that an organization execute very differently than what its current organizations structures, thinking, culture, and talent allow for. The current structures are set up to execute a plan today and change incrementally. However, the change for the future especially today requires a leap of faith and innovation that is difficult to operationalize. I cover this challenge in the chapter on Execution where we'll explore how to be ambidextrous – operate on both fronts at the same time.

For now, let's look at the 2 balancing perspectives of loyalty.

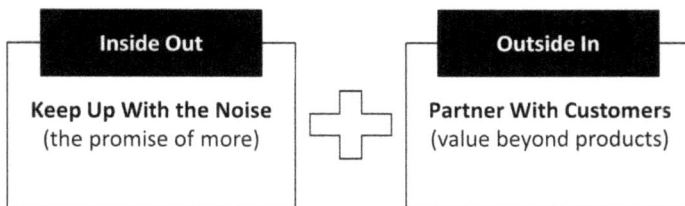

Inside Out

Keep Up With the Noise
(the promise of more)

Outside In

Partner With Customers
(value beyond products)

Fig: Two Balancing Perspective of Loyalty

Underlying both of these perspectives are the core elements of loyalty. These are also the ones most commonly used to improve and evolve our loyalty programs. A report by Capgemini also brought out several of these aspects (see ref 5).

- **More ways to earn points:** Going beyond purchases by awarding points and recognition for social interaction, brand community contributions, and product reviews
- **Ease of redeeming points:** Ensuring multi-channel redemption, easy look up of points and rewards, removing hurdles such as blackout dates
- **Quality of customer service:** Ensuring that questions are easily resolved, expectations are clear, and channels and agents are aware of the customer history and context
- **Expansive rewards catalog:** Constantly adjusting the rewards catalog to meet seasonal themes, as well as personalizing the offers based on analytics
- **More value for points or fees:** Ensuring that customer see immediate value in signing up or paying an upfront fee. Examples include Amazon's Prime program, higher tier airlines loyalty cards such as from United, as well as the seasonal high discount programs run by Citi, Discover, and others credit card companies. Often these programs are loss leaders but make up by driving up the volume of transactions to themselves or to their partners.

However, most loyalty programs in the market are leaning towards glorified promotional programs, something we will hopefully address through our 3 tier loyalty framework. A promotional or cash value based campaign strategy does have great uses. Some of them are:

- **Low hurdles to adoption** – Making it easier for customers to sign up through products or services that are initially free, and offer a paid upgrade to additional features (e.g. LinkedIn, PayPal, software Products, etc.)
- **Providing a trial period:** These are risk free trial periods for customers to experience the product or service (ISPs, fitness centers, etc) sometimes with an option to cancel without penalty, and often times with no upfront commitment as well.
- **Spurring demand:** Volume of transactions and acquisition of new customers can be improved through promotions and often pre-empting competition (Retail)
- **Cross sell subsidies:** These are also called loss leader strategies and are about offering a product or service at a low cost to pull customers in with the hope that they'll buy more of something that has a higher margin (Retail, Google, Facebook)
- Others

These are all methods that fall under the *Inside-Out* perspective of loyalty. Today, there are so many options available to customers that providing more ways to earn and redeem points is a step forward but is not enough. In addition, most programs in an industry are very similar in terms of what they offer. They are easily substituted and used.

In addition, customers remember to use the loyalty program when they transact after researching the best deal, not when they are planning to transact. This defeats the very purpose of loyalty and results in accumulation of points and redemption without actually boosting loyalty. Loyalty programs are seen as a way to earn point-in-time discounts, and there is almost no difference between new and existing members. This, even as marketing and promotions are stepped up.

Perhaps the most notable exceptions to this stark reality are the airlines rewards programs. The programs are tiered based on engagement. There are multiple gratification points built into various stages of the customer journey such as benefits during boarding, baggage, lounges, vacations, upgrades etc. The programs are longer term focused and have evolved over a long time thereby becoming very prominent in our lives – there are entire websites and businesses offering customers advice on how to maximize their miles, and which credit cards to get in order to do that. The programs have also established partnerships with other players such as banks and major retailers to improve distribution. In effect, they became an attractive channel for banks and retailers because customers could see every year the value these programs got them. They were easier to quantify (e.g. a family trip to the Caribbean) than simple cash back programs that are often capped at a similar value but represent a visible limit. An average person also dislikes mathematical calculations needed to compare the programs. Customers also have a "savings" tendency so it is psychologically easier to save towards a vacation rather than run the risk of spending the cash rewards too soon.

Another possible exception to commoditized loyalty programs – although in a different way - is the Amazon Prime program. The Prime program is a single entry point into free 2-day shipping, a vendor marketplace, access to the Kindle program, access to online TV, physical retail and grocery, the Amazon buy button, launch of the voice activated Alexa that is connecting banks and other players, and so much more. Amazon has built up a multipronged approach to provide exceptional value to Prime members. Profitability and self-selection remains a concern but who can possibly argue with the notion of world dominance. By looking at their share of retail spending in the US, and continuous innovations they come out with every day, one cannot argue with how Amazon is operating. At least for now, Amazon is doing everything right because they are turning established models on their heads, and it is difficult to catch up. They are winning today by demolition, and they are doing it across industries.

That brings us back to the core question *of getting customers to be loyal "despite" price premiums, and building long term & profitable relationships.* In a connected world, the definition of loyalty has to be more customer-centric and focused on customer aspirations and experiences. The airline loyalty programs started with miles but soon became a means for families to bring dream destinations and trips within grasp, not to mention better travel experiences for frequent flyers. Similarly, American Express made possible early access to concerts of our favorite celebrities and popular Broadway shows. It also provided exclusive service during travel. These were programs that changed the perception of value they delivered. The translation of spending to value was made complicated, and in some cases impossible.

We'll use some of those constructs and concepts to build out the 3-Tier loyalty model that can serve as a good reference model for the future of loyalty.

The 3-Tier Model of Loyalty in a Connected World

Let's now look at the 3-tiered model of loyalty to address the Outside-In – aka customer centric – perspective of loyalty programs. The 3 tiers are aligned to the kinds of value we can provide our customers. Subsequently, we will explore how this fundamental 3-Tier model will function in a connected world.

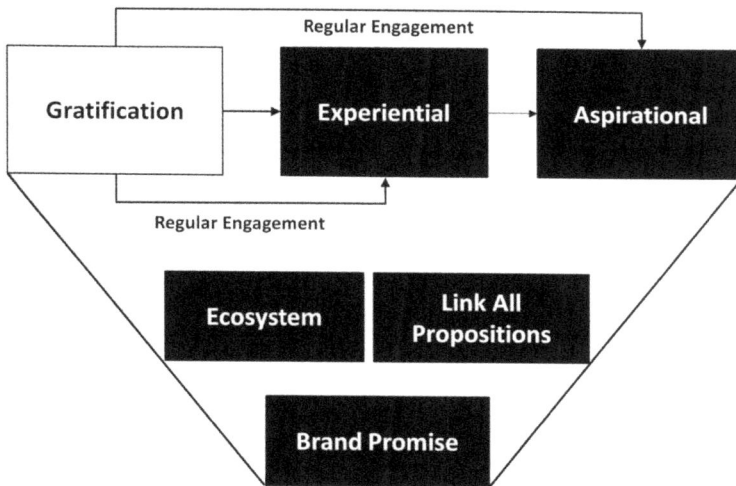

Fig: The 3-Tiered Loyalty Model

Too often we see loyalty as a way to earn points and spur the next transaction. But there's a lot under the hood. I designed the 3-tiered loyalty model to re-examine the popular concept of loyalty so that it becomes a strategic discussion, not just a supporting activity.

Tier 1 of the model elevates the cash and discount model to create experiences and aspirations for customers. The reason to do that is simple. We need a way to align the brand promise with the way customers interact with us. Points and discounts are a common way to "reward" customers. It is indeed gratifying to see the total amount on the bill magically shed cents and dollars at the cash counter. All that is needed is to sign up for a loyalty program. However, it is increasingly obvious that points and discounts are becoming table stakes. A 2015 brand loyalty study indicated that 76% of Americans think that loyalty programs are part of their relationship with brands (see ref 6). Heartening as that number seems, we must also delve deeper into what makes them say that - do they actually mean they won't shop at your brand if you don't offer them cash discounts, or do they receive something they cannot get elsewhere? The same study (see ref 6) also pointed out that 44% of surveyed customers believe that it'll be easy to switch one rewards program with another, and 67% will change the brands they purchase to maximize their benefits from transactions. This implies that we are operating at a much commoditized level with our loyalty programs. The issue is broader than just points and rewards. Instead this is a strategic topic about the differentiation we enjoy in the customers' minds.

Tier 2 is meant to leverage the power of an ecosystem of players which may be from many different industries. Every business has channels they reach customers on. However, the concept of ecosystems tries to understand the complementary or supplementary needs that our products are a part of. And that means striking up partnerships with other businesses that lead to our business. For example, a clothing retailer may partner with an events company, or with a firm offering outdoor adventures. A casual dining restaurant may partner with fitness centers or local retailers to deliver an all-in-one package. American Express recently made Uber rides possible and rewarded through its mobile app. Technology make all of this possible today. And if we don't think and act strategically to build connections between different value propositions, someone else will beat us to it. Tier 2 is all about putting the customer, not our products, at the center of the universe.

Tier 3 brings the core brand promise at the forefront of the loyalty discussion so that every action reinforces the emotional and physical contract we intend to establish with our customers. We often think of how seamless it must be for customers to sign up and redeem their points. But is seamless the right way for us to build true loyalty? Should we instead keep loyalty prominent but make the actual transactions seamless. It ranges from business process simplification to customer experience tactics.

- First there are the differentiation aspects such as being the first to come to mind when customers not only think of the core products, but also complementary activities (as in the ecosystem we build). The question to ask is whether our loyalty program a is part of their decision making process when customers are looking for our products or evaluating their overall need which our product is a part of. For example Panera Bread recently moved to being 100% clean food with no artificial ingredients and preservatives. This development gives them the foundation to develop the other capabilities. Our products are a core foundation of our brand promise. Customers need proof points and satisfaction that the brand is living up to its promise.

- Second, we must think of process issues - how easy is it for consumers to track and redeem, do they know how their program works, how do the rewards link to our brand, what do customers feel and how they talk about our service. Order ahead and pick up services from Starbucks are a great example of how they remove friction from the process. The emergence of Apple Pay is another example – in addition to higher security, mobile payment is seamless and convenient. Amazon Prime is another example of friction being demolished. The entire industry is ripe with examples of how friction is being removed. The major difference between the approaches take by companies is this: do we look inside-out from our products perspective (e.g. Panera), or do we look outside-in to build an ecosystem (e.g. American Express Plenti). Both approaches are needed to be considered. Ultimately, the outside-in approach is a must to be considered. The outside-in approach builds additional competitive barriers and additional customer engagement avenues.

- Third, we need to think of how we connect emotional connections with physical experiences, and how do customers directly experience our brand with the promise it projects. For example, if customers buy outfits for an outdoor adventure, are we forgotten after the purchase? Think of Panera for a minute. How does it reinforce the 100% clean food brand with physical experiences after the purchase. The ecosystems of external companies we are beginning to create in a connected world offers us new avenues to reinforce our brand promise. In addition, fear of how a partner may negatively impact our brand through adverse experiences for no fault of ours is very real, but it's a risk we must take on and mitigate if we wish to become relevant in a connected world.

All three tiers of the loyalty model are interconnected, and must be considered together as we set about creating a strong customer engagement and loyalty program. In a connected, digital world, our business models are being transformed every day in unexpected ways. The 3-tier model of loyalty helps us create lasting relationships, by thinking beyond points and miles.

Let's now look at the 3 Tiers in more detail.

Tier 1: Moving Towards Experiences and Aspirations

At the top tier, the loyalty model depicted above creates rewards that go beyond discounts and promotions to engage customers in a long term conversation about their needs, inspirations, and motivations.

Today, **gratification** is the most commonly adopted definition of loyalty programs. At this level we offer more points, more easily, through more avenues for immediate tangible value such as discounts, cash backs, free coffees, free haircuts, free shipping and so on. This delivered value is the foundation of a loyalty program, and required to keep up customer engagement with regular offers for point redemption. The gratification model is so universal that a significant part of the discussion today about loyalty is about how we are innovating to boost this earn-points-and-redeem model. Almost every retailer offers such a program, and they must do to initiate their loyalty management journey. However, as we saw earlier in this chapter, research shows that (see ref 4 and 6):

1. Customer engagement is sorely lacking despite all the points being racked up, and despite all of the discounts available to customers
2. Further, customers treat brands like fungible resources, willing to switch at the next better incentive that shows up

What we need additionally at this level are measures that keep up contextual customer engagement and anticipation of benefits by customers.

Consider a sample scenario for contextual customer engagement. A clothing retailer may provide us coupons and discount codes for our next purchase. What makes the difference is how it keeps in touch with us with context based offers that spur us to redeem those rewards, and earn additional rewards for our next purchase. If we purchase winter coats, can we be drawn into the store for winter boots, or for spring shopping? This ability to maintain a memory of the customer's relationship needs to be built if we hope to engage our customers. Sending millions of mass emails and being happy about conversion rates is not going to cut it.

Consider another scenario of how anticipation of benefits can be set up. A casual coffee and food house such as Panera or Starbucks may offer us rewards and points in terms of free coffee, pastries etc. First, they could remind us at every purchase what we have available to redeem in the upcoming weeks so our future choices are positively influenced in their favor. To build on that tactic, building up of customer context plays a role. Can they draw us into stores at occasions to which our minds automatically link these products? For example, winter and coffee, or a relaxing summer afternoon spent reading a book? In addition, such places have opportunities to successfully build up customer context by asking questions on why we are there. Most of us frequent these locations to work, or read a book, meet up with friends or business contacts, and for an occasional lunch with family. These locations only need to ask us why we are there, and then with our permission, develop appropriate workflows to invite us in. Similar scenarios can be constructed for almost any business – consider Uber or Lyft, hotels, restaurants, spas, banks, auto repair, insurance, and so on. Our interactions can be time triggered to start with, and then set to fire on context as soon as we are able to build the context.

The next level up in the loyalty is the **experiential level.** This level helps customers feel differentiated and exclusive. The experiential level is less commonly adopted because it is more difficult to operationalize. It provides rewards that are less about money, and more about exclusivity and experiences. At this level, the program trades some portion of the immediate gratification value towards bragging and feel good rights. Examples include concierge services such as free personalized valet parking for your next date, the reserved corner table for dinner at an exclusive restaurant, early access to concert tickets, the red carpet to boarding the flight, etc. One can probably put a monetary value to these rewards, but the value delivered is way beyond money. At this level, customers begin to feel more exclusive as these experiences are unique to those at this level, and must be earned. Apart from beginning to create a relationship with customers, this level also improves the loyalty economics by reducing the cost of redemptions. It takes the focus away from monetary value, because the perceived value is subjective and differs greatly from customer to customer.

Consider the examples from the previous section, and we can begin to see how experiences can begin to be created. Early preview of new clothing inventory, reserving items based on preferences, notifying that a table has been reserved, or the meal automatically ordered if customers are to come in are examples of experiential perks that customers can brag about. These are not available to everyone. These are not commoditized.

As before, reinforcement of these experiences is needed. In addition, we offer many benefits to our customers today which we don't brand and reinforce appropriately. For example, most banks today offer such exclusive features such as refunding ATM fees arising from out-of-network ATM usage. But banks don't always tell the customers of this important action they've taken. The fees are quietly refunded after a few days. This is a bragging right that both banks and customers must have. Instead, what customers hear most about are unfair fees charged by banks. Similarly, notifications of how a retirement fund is performing and offers of a free review with customers are overshadowed by sales messages. As a result these are not welcomed by customers. Instead, these interactions should be branded as exclusive customer service for exclusive customers because that's what these really are.

The final level in the tier 1 is about **aspirations.** This level of the loyalty model further helps customers positively make choices in our favor given multiple other options. This level is fantastic to get customers in a state of working with you on a long term goal that they aspire or journey towards. Aspirational loyalty is linked to and emerges from the experiential level. The primary difference stems from creating a longer term motivation for customers that cannot just be measured in monetary terms. At this level the program will structure regular redemptions but gear itself towards setting a higher goal as well.

We often associate airline loyalty programs with aspirations. But any firm can embark on this journey. For this, we need to look beyond our products and examine the customers' motivations. Example include building towards a family trip to the Bahamas, saving for the dream home, sending a child to college, status in the community as "The Social Citizen" etc. Fitness is another global theme. Who doesn't aspire to this noble but challenging goal?

Thus, the three levels in the top tier of the loyalty model progressively elevate and transform conversations from being about us and our products, to being about customers and their aspirations. That is a much needed progression in today's connected world. When we go to the next tier in the loyalty model, we'll see how building an ecosystem makes this easier to conceive and execute.

As digital technology evolves to make it easier for businesses to innovate on their business processes, this 3 step model of gratification-experience-aspirations is no longer the domain of large enterprises with deep pockets. In fact, the innovations are not new. Almost all large brands of yesterday such as American Express and Citi, had built experiential and aspirational aspects of their loyalty programs. They provided membership benefits such as early access to exclusive concerts and planning for vacations.

The vision of brands such as Citi and American Express gave rise to a lot of specialist providers that sprang up to meet these needs – concert tickets, concierge services, travel planning etc. Many of those specialist service providers have now evolved to provide services in a broader way to other brands who might want to leverage this model. In addition, what has also made this new model easier to operationalize is the rise of the sharing economy, internet based platforms, and the API model (where software applications of one company can be invoked by another). There is now no need to embark on capital intensive IT programs today to launch a new business capability. What is needed instead is a solid business sense and vision to move the organization forward in a way that is different from today.

A good example of how a loyalty program can extend beyond the inside-out model and bring a focus on customers is how Walgreens is rewarding customer actions on related health themes (see ref 31). Points are linked to broader health and fitness activities thereby opening up the model to a potentially large ecosystem of industry and cross-industry players. This loyalty program model has the potential now to include the 2 core pillars of the business previously executed separately – retail and pharmacy. In addition, by linking into the Plenti program by American Express, the boundaries of the program can be developed further. Plenti has created a program across a wide set of industry players thus connecting customer needs across the participating companies. There is still much work to be done but the evolution is a step in the right direction. We'll look another look at the Plenti program later in this chapter.

The 3-tiered model of loyalty takes us beyond immediate cash discounts – gratification value – and avoids manifesting the tendency of customers to perceive an ever-lower price to value tradeoff. Further, in a rapidly evolving digital marketplace, maintaining customer engagement should be top priority. The progression from Gratification-Experience-Aspiration can be leveraged to slowly transform our programs to be focused squarely on the customer. As we align better with our customers' broader ecosystems, incremental wins in customer engagement will also help stay ahead of disruptive innovations.

Tier 2: Ecosystems and Linking All propositions

In this tier, we will examine how the loyalty model can be linked strategically to the core differentiation that is developed through cross-industry partnerships, and by focusing on the customer.

Competition in a connected world comes from unexpected sources.

- MasterCard and Visa are threatened today by mobile P2P payments that tend to use banking direct debit models instead of relying on the credit card networks alone (see ref 21). A few years ago anyone trying to build such a direct debit payment model would face an uphill battle. In fact, the market need for seamless payments and application of credit is precisely how the credit card networks rose to prominence. Over time they did well to create partnerships and loyalty models to innovate and provide additional customer value. It can be argued that the convenience in payments also came at a social cost of a credit burdened society. But these network models were also instrumental in developing benchmarks of financial credit worthiness which serve us well even today. Now, with the emergence of smartphones and digital technology, new and innovative competing payments models are coming faster to market. They are also able to quickly attain critical mass by piggybacking on the very model they intend to disrupt. The business agreements that Visa and MasterCard entered into with PayPal are an illustration of how the new payment models can quickly disrupt this widely accepted ecosystem of credit cards networks.

- In addition, the recent two hour shipping and delivery phenomenon is affecting major players like FedEx and UPS, who also have to reckon with innovative delivery methods such as use of drones, and shipping via peer-to-peer networks in a shared economy model (see ref 32). The popularity of services such as Uber and Lyft is opening up yet another model for delivery that completely bypasses traditional shipping providers.

- In the financial world, Bitcoin is poised to transform the very definition of currency, and makes government regulation difficult by opening up a completely unregulated model of value transfer. Governments and banks can regulate money, but how would they regulate flow of value (see ref 33)?

In times like these, innovating on products, enhancing customer engagement, and building loyalty is critical to compete. It is natural, but also counter-intuitive for us to hunker down and adopt the push and sell model of our traditional value propositions. There is little doubt that factors such as quality, being first to market, user adoption and customer perception are really important. Amazon, Google, Apple, Cloudera, and Facebook are great examples of how these have allowed them to surge ahead. But *advances in digital now almost mandate that we strategically think* of what else we can do to generate stickiness with customers, and in turn generate "loyalty". That enhanced loyalty will come from:

1. Identifying the weak links in our customer engagement
2. Filling the white spaces in our product value propositions

3. Evolving the very definition of what loyalty means in a networked world.

Digital disruption is a term not to be taken lightly, because we have seen – in the past several years alone – so many established and well respected players fell from grace due to inertia and inaction.

This 2nd tier of the loyalty model focuses on product innovation. There are two imperative as we analyze the question of customer intimacy, differentiation and loyalty. The following will help as a starting point with the customer at the center of our universe and building ecosystems to expand the value of what we deliver.

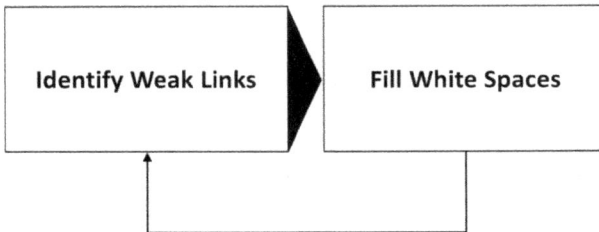

Fig: Steps To Evolve Loyalty Models

Identify the weak links

What relates us to the customer? How are we connected to the customer today? Are we taking these links for granted?

For example, banks relied on consumer pulling out their credit cards for payments. Now consumers pull out their phone and use Apple Pay. Some major retailers are offering a robust 5% off if a store card is used. Are banks invisible? Has the banking relationship taken a back seat? It can be argued that these are new channels for the trusted banking relationship to expand. But customers are increasingly looking at their bank as undifferentiated suppliers of core services. About 53% of customers in this millennials oriented study (see ref 34) find their banks to be undifferentiated. These banking core services are at present difficult for others to provide. But gradually with the rise of online only bank holding companies such as American Express, Goldman Sachs, PayPal and many other emerging startups such as Fidor in Germany, and Atom in the UK, large portions of liquid capital is moving steadily to these providers. The incentive for customers is higher interest rates, same government guarantees on deposits, and the ability to still be able to access their money almost as conveniently as before. Yes, there are still limitations in the new model, but traditional banks should evaluate whether those limitations are commonplace enough, and strong enough, to hold back this momentum gathering trend. In short, core services are being commoditized, so what else can they offer while they still have the advantages of incumbency?

Similarly the sharing economy is completely usurping the traditional models of customer outreach. There are no longer service providers directly working with their customers. Instead, a new wave of intermediaries is creating all kinds of marketplaces to sell all kinds of products and services. In the early stages, middlemen such as Priceline.com were actually a new channel for hospitality providers to sell unused or surplus inventory, and these channels appealed to certain niche cases. However, the emergence of end user brokers such as Airbnb is inspiring competitive models. Today Airbnb seems to be serving spare rooms at a budget, but they are rapidly moving towards creating highly thematic vacations for families as well.

Dis-intermediation and disruption are the technical terms for this broad phenomenon. They may not be received very well, and even actively resisted, in management board rooms, but the underlying trends must be acknowledged and addressed. Every disruption starts small and seems to be limited to a niche. But over time the models evolve to become mainstream and directly competitive. Identification of weak links is a crucial activity. And it cannot be done by resisting the new realities.

To identify the weak links, we must ask these questions among others:

1. What could be replacing or substituting our engagement with customers regarding our core value propositions? E.g. hotels, payments, bank accounts, insurance policies, lending, retail, vacations, and almost everything.
2. What is the additional value that customers find in these new engagements? E.g. ease of use, less cost, faster time to complete, more options, wider variety of products etc.

Some of answers to the above questions are obvious. And sometimes we don't want to see them. The first and most crucial step is to acknowledge and understand.

Fill the white spaces

In the previous section on identifying weak links, we saw how to identify emerging gaps in how we meet our customer's needs. This second step of filling in the white spaces consists of understanding customers' identities and taking steps to meet evolving needs. Filling white spaces is a two pronged challenge of core product innovation and creation of partnerships.

On the other hand, the backdrop of our strategy in the recent past has been about our core business and expanding channels and distribution. Loyalty models have been offered as a means to encourage transactions. In the new connected world that strategy needs to be turned on its head. Loyalty can no longer be an add-on of points and discounts. It must be integrated tightly with what we offer to our clients. In other words, the silos that made execution easier have to be demolished if are to compete effectively.

In the pre-connected era, customers have had to look to multiple players in well defined, independent industries to meet the spectrum of their needs – through another product, service or channel. Core product and service innovation are often used to address latent customer needs that are closely tied to a product or service. For example research on product fitment prior to purchase was performed either independently or through specialized third parties. Services that complement the product were also purchased separately (e.g. wires or plugs for an electronic device, bill payments for bank customers, etc.) Similarly, post-sales service was purchased separately. As part of product innovation, these immediate and obvious extensions of the core experience are brought inside the fold so we can control – and profit from – these transactions. Loyalty models were enhanced to include transactions and rewards related to these core product innovations.

While product innovations were a great idea, the world is getting connected so fast, that a single business will probably never be able to compete with emerging ecosystems. The solution is to build out a friendly chain of links with other industry players – in other words a partnership ecosystem. For example, when customers look to see if a product meets their needs, do they ask you or a third party? When customers walk into a retail store, what triggered that need? When they are looking at available discounts on their bank's mobile app, are those offers relevant to what they need? A study of the weak links as in the previous section will lead us to generate these insights.

Not all businesses, especially smaller businesses, will think that they have the resources to envision and execute on this approach. In a technology first world it almost looks like making massive technology investments is a first step towards evolution. But it doesn't have to be. In fact, local business level partnerships may actually be a better way to create, target and test the propositions. Today most of the core underlying technology pieces are already in place. Every business, however small has a web presence today. And the sharing economy has made it possible for large brands to be developed from the comfort of one's home. Almost all businesses have untapped partners in the form of services through APIs from product firms and service institutions such as banks, retailers and insurers. In addition, niche bloggers and even the local YMCA can bring communities of people together. These partners are looking to expand and establish themselves as well.

The key is to identify potential weak links in our value chain, and move towards addressing them. In today's world, it's easy to be disinter-mediated, so partnerships that expand our relationships also protect our customer engagement avenues. Such partners are also best positioned to channel our experiential and aspirational rewards. Partnerships set up the foundation for the experiential and aspirational tiers of our loyalty program.

Let's take the example of a fictitious children's clothing retailer. At different times of the year, the retailer comes up with new lines, designs and brands that are aimed at meeting the seasonal needs, as well as create differentiation from its competitors. It creates online tools where customers can see how the clothes look on their children. It advertises on various channels where customers are likely to be, provides heavy discount codes for old inventory, creates time bound promotions for the new inventory, and links the purchases to a loyalty card. The loyalty card drives repeat purchases based on additional discounts, volume of purchases, and referrals to other customers. The offers are sent out by mass email as well, and sometimes the email campaigns are targeted and segmented. This retailer is doing everything right – at least from a traditional perspective. If it can do these actions well, they should be very happy. However, the potential of the connected, digital world is largely untapped. For example, it knows that children have different activities they pursue in different seasons (sports, outdoors, birthdays, etc.), but it doesn't tap into that information, or doesn't have it. It doesn't work directly with the providers of those services to children. Moreover, the retailer doesn't interact with the providers of services to their parents who may have favorite brands of their own and may pursue hobbies and activities of their own. When customers come in, it doesn't have information to personalize their visits based on their wish-lists they might have set. It has home delivery options, but it doesn't use that to drive predetermined purchase of staples which it knows are coming for sure.

Let's face it. A lot of what was outlined in the previous paragraph can be summed up in this way: *The retailer does the inside-out very well, but it lags on the outside-in momentum.* In fact, one of the most common reasons cited for retailer personalization is privacy. But, as I've said before, we may have privacy backwards. We are unable to meet privacy norms because we lack customer engagement, not vice versa. Everything I stated in the example above can be done with explicit customer consent and engagement. Customers are looking for value. Of course we have to safeguard the data we collect, but we are doing that today as well.

It is definitely prudent to focus on the core operations and to keep the cash registers ringing. But a sole focus on inside-out results in disruption if we also don't take steps to consider the outside-in. We need to fill the white spaces, because industry innovations are making sure that information will be leveraged to stamp out any advantages that arise from commoditized plays. The same is true of all other industries. We've seen fintechs make banks seem like dinosaurs, insurers playing the pricing game, airlines trying to scale to reduce costs because they can't increase their pie, taxis as we know them are on the way out, and so on. Equally important are innovations such as with Internet of Things and autonomous machines (e.g. cars) that will make new ways to engage customers critical because the existing entry points for product considerations and purchase will close dramatically.

Customers are always going to have needs that go beyond what we are engaging with them for. But it doesn't mean that we step back from the scene. The 3-tiered structure of loyalty helps us carry customer engagement beyond organizational boundaries.

For example, Horizon Blue Cross Blue Shield of NJ created a program (see ref 1) where the time spent at Lifetime Fitness would yield benefits for this customer at both businesses. The loyalty program "Plenti" is also tapping into this concept by joining together multiple businesses such as American Express, Macy's and Exxon Mobile. In addition to businesses joining hands, customers can enter into partnerships too to maximize the value of their points. Somewhat similar to Amazon Prime, Costco is constantly adding an entire ecosystem of service providers such as home furnishing to their core membership. The Giant Eagle Fuel Perks programs was a smashing early success because people saved for their weekly fill-up, linked various types of purchases to this program and saw the savings climbing up at the gas pump. Apparently there's something about indirect gratification, and people actually spread the word by linking status to it as well – "We get good fuel for less because we're a member". Same is true of airline miles programs – folks have been known to fly to earn points to maintain status, even when not needed.

Building ecosystems and linking the value propositions we can offer will also move us towards aspirational or experiential rewards in a connected world. These models are stickier and more engaging. Creating partnerships and filling out white spaces gives us the ability to do so. Tapping into activities that partners are performing allows us to not only engage with our customers who are already involved with a partner's activity, but it allows our partners to engage those customers who we can reach out to on their behalf. It's a win-win. For example, if a retailer has an event at a farmer's market, fitness centers can leverage the event to engage joint customers who may not already be involved. In fact, without being tightly integrated with technology, these cross-partner loyalty programs can still add tremendous value when it comes to customer engagement. To encourage exclusive experiential events such as concerts, guided museum trips, fun vacations among other things, multiple partners can come together to define common scoring criteria which can be implemented using simple digital tools. These experiences can then be tied to aspirations and goals that members work towards.

In addition, experiential and aspirational nature of the rewards supported by ecosystems allows us to reduce the cost of redemption. The timeless MasterCard tagline illustrates that beautifully: "There are some things money can't buy. For everything else, there's MasterCard". For a basketball fan, an on-court encounter with LeBron James may be something they dream of but can probably never achieve. Same goes for in-kitchen experience with Chef Emeril for many of his fans. But for sponsors who own the loyalty program, providing this opportunity to their diehard fans may not be too complex or expensive. Scenarios like these are fairly common, and with the connected 3-tier model of loyalty, these can be very easily developed.

Tier 3 – Brand Promise

Where do core products and offerings fit in? The value of a core product propositions cannot be overemphasized. Underlying everything else are the brand promise we project to our customers, and the utility we provide. There are 2 ways to do that:

1. **Providing products and services that customers need but haven't received yet:** All new innovations falls under this category – The iPhone, Uber and Lyft, Airbnb, LinkedIn, PayPal and Venmo, Apple Pay, Paytm and Alipay, Amazon's Alexa, Netflix, Amazon Prime, Amazon's hosting services, Tesla, and so on. A novel product that provides untapped utility takes us a long way and often disrupts the industry. It spurs traditional competitors to action. And when competitors do start catching up, everyone knows that constant innovation keep us ahead. But innovation alone doesn't guarantee success in today's connected and rapidly evolving market. That's where the second point below comes into play.

2. **Ecosystems and integration of value propositions:** Every successful proposition today is connected in various ways to enhance the core value, and to create a formidable barrier to its competitors. Those who are not doing it are on the path to commoditization even if that path is not obvious. As we have discussed, and as we will see again in the chapters on Integration and customer engagement, ecosystems means finding new ways to bring cross industry value together. Almost all of the innovations listed in the previous paragraph are attempting to link to products we wouldn't

have thought they would link to. Take almost any product that doesn't connect to others today and its survival is dubious at best - waiting for a better mousetrap to disrupt it. Amazon's Alexa is gaining adoption because it brings service providers like banks and retailers together. It creates a channel to reach customers. The same is true of Apple. And in the coming months we'll see new ways in which others are doing the same. Uber is already a channel for financial investment firms, Tesla can be a marketplace platform as well, and so can PayPal if they do it right.

Why did we reach the conclusion that connected is the only way forward. Because that's the only way we can think outside-in and be focused on the customer, rather than on what we alone have to offer. And only by doing so, our brands are aligned to customer purpose, and integrate expectations with physical experiences.

That's why the final tier holding up the loyalty model is about brand promise. The brand promise guides not only how we will play in the market, but also makes our value propositions focused solely on the customers. Our customers are buying products, but they are – after all is said and done - meeting a need. Our products are but a small part of that overall need. For example, we buy high quality sound systems, but our need is broader. The brands that understand this are creating integrations and partnerships to bring us that end to end experience. Others are focused on creating high quality speakers alone. They will definitely have their place, until someone sweeps the rug from under their feet. Like what is happening to physical retail stores and banks. And like what might happen to Uber and Lyft when self-driving cars from manufacturers make a direct play and offer amazing options to customers. It's mostly conjecture of course, but not far-fetched. It'll be very interesting and exciting to see how all this will play out.

Thus, our brand promise is the one we should focus on first by thinking outside-in - starting with the customer. It will reflect our strategy for competing in the future. It will lead to creation of ecosystems, and finally lead to creating experiences and meeting the aspirations of our customers. And while we do that, it will leave in its wake solid hurdles and barriers for our competition.

As we think of what our brand stands for, the 3-tier loyalty model will also be enabled by a couple of other aspects we'll consider as we go along in this book.

First, we need to make our brand promise real. When customers hear our brand slogans on how we trust them, or make them happy, or satisfy their spirit of adventure, it does various things. First, it establishes an emotional connect in the customers' minds. We start associating our feelings with the brand. That's one of the reasons we see Coca Cola winning when rational taste tests indicate otherwise. There's also a pre-conditioning effect which leads customers to prefer a brand that establishes the connection. It leads to inertia in customers in a good way. But over time, as the products get commoditized, the brand promise starts fading, or disillusionment creeps in. Information asymmetry has helped us so far, but in a connected and digital world, it is critical to reinforce the brand promise through physical interactions.

The question to ask is this: what can we do to support the promises our brand makes? In my first book, I called this *The*

Principle of Customer Interaction. It's all about linking the emotional with the physical. For example, a retailer that promises confidence should reinforce that post purchase as well, and a bank that conveys trust and confidence should show how it actually does that. The techniques are diverse but we can start with reassurances to customers and prospects, or simple show & tell as we continue our journey with them. Without that our brand gets lost in the me-too crowd.

Second, being connected is all about bringing the focus on purpose of customers, rather than solely on our products. A brand promise that starts with that automatically paves the way for creating the vision that drives operational execution. For example, a brand that focuses on health, finds ways to connect the various players together in its journey towards being connected. These players can be fitness centers, retailers, local farmers, sporting goods companies, restaurants, doctors, nutritionists and a multitude of other players focused on health in their own narrow way, but each needed to make up the whole. Thus we need to expand the brand promise to beyond our own products.

In short, we must look outside-in.

The correct brand promise drives ecosystems and value propositions. And in turn those items drive the rewards program to start becoming experiential and aspirational. Not only is that good for loyalty economics, but it's good for the health of our companies too, not to mention our customers.

Summary

The means to achieve loyalty and differentiation are easier and at the same time more complicated in today's digital and connected world. We can reach customers quickly and universally. The question to ask is: are we starting this encounter with a discount offer or are we engaging with customers in a slow dance for a longer term ecosystem?

Almost all businesses have multiple services and products. If we consider our total relationship with customers, we may have much more value to exchange. Most recently, Amazon is leveraging the Prime membership to not only cover shipping, but also including media (movies etc.) streaming, as well as the Kindle Unlimited reading program. More than just bringing together the value of the total relationship, this approach also helps establish customer centricity from the top down. Consider our banks and insurers as candidates for this model. Even as community banks tell us they are closer to the community, do we see the proof points? Are they easily accessible? How about reinforcing customer choices after the transaction is done with service & marketing coming together. Relationship based businesses do this almost intuitively. American Express perhaps decided to project exclusivity and luxury with its early access program. Amazon could be signaling unlimited choice, while Walgreen's is probably on its way to signaling partnership in health.

The 3-tier connected loyalty model ultimately helps connect brand promises to overall customer needs and physical experiences. In a world flooded with information, it is difficult to weed through to the true value behind a product or offer. How do we give weight to our claims – prove that they are true. Our brands project strong emotional sentiments such as security, comfort, luxury, or reliability among others. Our loyalty programs should support those values and bring them to life. Creating ecosystems, integrating propositions, providing experiential and aspirational rewards is a way to identify physical interactions that will complement the customers' emotional engagement with our brands.

BLOCK 3: CUSTOMER ENGAGEMENT

The connected model of Customer Engagement shows us how emotional and physical engagement touchpoints should and can complement each other. It also shows how to reinforce customer confidence in our brand so we can become a reference anchor in our customers' minds by being an advice engine.

In Block 1, we discussed how customer personas and customer journeys must cross the boundaries of our own products and services. In this chapter we'll see how to action those personas and journeys.

In a connected world, the notion of customer engagement must be revisited because the parameters of engagement have dramatically changed. We've come a long way since the days when customer engagement used to be about simple metrics such as number of touch-points, share of mind, traffic, and click through rates. Recent advances in measurement of customer engagement have highlighted new parameters such as referrals, net promoter score, and loyalty, among others. Most recently as I highlighted in *Dancing The Digital Tune*, customer engagement is about connecting the emotional brand promises with physical interactions, and creating trust. And now, moving forward in a connected world, customer engagement must be measured in terms of stickiness of the ecosystem. In fact, the entire cycle of measurement will follow a similar evolution curve but will be measured instead by how we perform in an ecosystem.

The following figure highlights this parallel track of establishing and measuring customer engagement. And the rest of this chapter will examine how to execute as per this new paradigm.

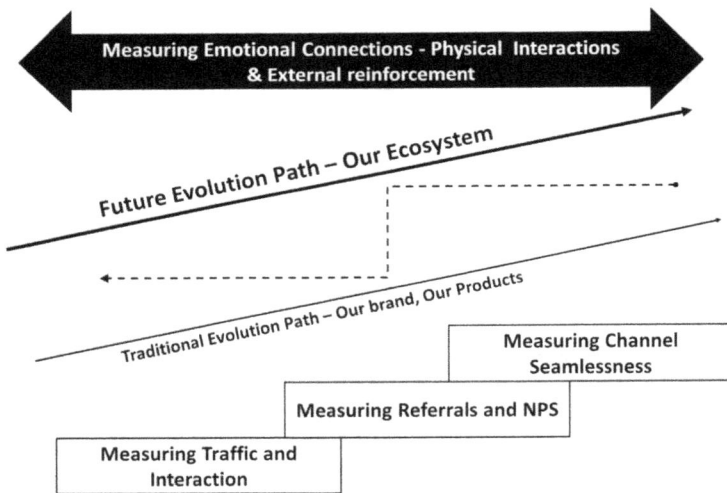

Fig: The New Context of Customer Engagement - Ecosystems

The new path of evolution offers hope that we do not have to unlearn everything. The traditional expertise can still be leveraged to compete in the new economy. But as history has repeatedly demonstrated, the speed of adaptation is critical.

Those who will understand this model and embrace it quickly will outperform those who don't. Time has always been an equalizer, but in today's rapidly changing and innovating marketplace, that may not be so because new customer habits are formed quicker than ever. Therefore, the passage of time may actually make it more difficult to restore parity until the next market disruption occurs. We do not have to look beyond the successes of new taxi companies such as Uber, Ola, and Lyft, and new hospitality companies such as Airbnb to drive home this point. When customers get used to an experience, it is difficult to switch them away unless either the market becomes commoditized or until the next disruption comes across. And with the power of digital and internet today, both of these factors are on the side of innovators, not slow movers.

Let's now look at what I consider to be the two bulwarks of customer engagement in the future, and then examine how they can be leveraged in a connected economy.

- Linking emotional connections with physical customer interactions
- Fulfilling the need for external reinforcement

Revisiting the Customer Interaction Index

In *Dancing The Digital Tune*, I had outlined a simple way of measuring the strength of our customer interactions. The model depicts a continuum where customers move between emotional connections with a brand and actual physical interactions through buying and customer service. All brands operate at both ends of this spectrum.

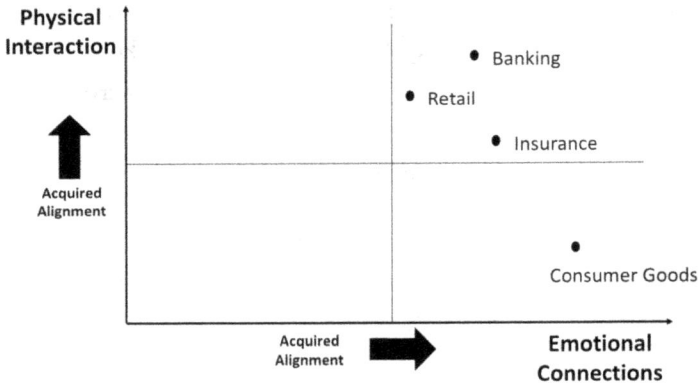

Fig: Representative Natural Customer Interaction Index of Some Common Industries

The Customer Interaction Index performs two functions. First, it outlines a simple method to understand what our inherent interaction model for customer engagement is. For example, some transaction heavy industries such as banking have a higher customer interaction index because they interact at a personal level. They are at an inherent advantage when it comes to tying the emotional and physical ends of the spectrum together. Likewise, some consumer product oriented organizations are lower when it comes to the inherent customer interaction index, and rely on emotional branding. Their capacity to interact and engage at a personal and individual level is limited.

Second, the Customer Interaction Index helps us develop a roadmap to deeper customer engagement by identifying mechanisms that will connect the emotional and physical ends of the spectrum. For example, banks can connect the emotional promise of financial security by providing reinforcement through physical interactions of how they are actually doing it.

Firms always connect with customers at both physical and emotional levels. In a connected digital world, we must increasingly interlink and reinforce the two ends of the spectrum – emotional and physical. This must be done to stay relevant, in a way that's right for the firm and its customers. The capabilities that we develop must be aligned as per that strategy. How well the two ends of the spectrum converge indicates how deep the customer engagement is. That's because technology has leveled the playing field. How we want customers to perceive us is now intricately linked to how customers actually experience our brand (not just in advertising or positioning, but during transactions and customer service).

It is important to measure how we are reinforcing the emotional messaging that attracts our customers. For examples, if we portray exclusivity, respect and honesty, then are we providing the same undifferentiated and mechanized physical interaction experience to our customers? When we walk into a bank, or use their services, is there really a difference between banks in how we trust them? Likewise, is there really a difference between how one luxury retailer behaves compared to another, or are their products differentiated too? In addition, do they follow through after the transaction to reinforce their brands? The dramatic effects of failure to connect emotional and physical interactions reflect in poor customer engagement. Promotions and discounts must be constantly used to get customers to engage. In short, slogans and branding tactics won't cut it anymore in a connected world where customers have easy access to information, and the power to choose.

This customer engagement model changes the perspective because it refers to a different kind of strategy. There's really no other choice today. Our goal is to have experiences drive transactions and vice versa. The impact of this principle can be seen from the enormous amounts being spent on advertising and promotions today to raise awareness and getting customers to experience the products.

So using this simple measurement tool, we can now think about identifying:

- How can firms who rely on emotional connect also increase their index on the physical 1-1 relationships?
- How do firms who are high on 1-1 interaction also progress on the emotional connections with customers?

It follows that the capabilities needed are not just digital. Our customer service channels, sales outlets, brokers, agents, distributors etc. all need to come together. I explored this concept in detail in *Dancing The Digital Tune*.

Revisiting External Reinforcement

In *Dancing The Digital Tune,* I outlined another principle that focused on external reinforcement. That principle highlighted how we need to address all aspects of the customer journey in order to secure a trusted position for our brands. It highlighted the simple fact that customer engagement remains incomplete if we focus only on our products and services. Customers are looking for validation and reinforcement at every stage. They turn to many different sources to fulfill that need. And we give up control of their decision making process by not stepping forward and addressing that need head on.

Look at the illustration that depicts the cycle of external reinforcement. We'll notice how we cater to the top half of the customer engagement process, but largely ignore the below.

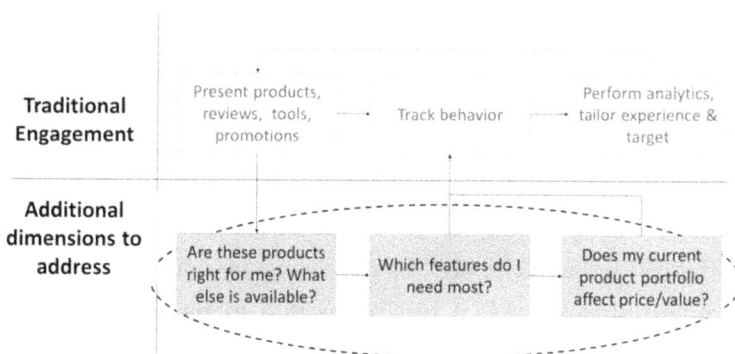

Fig: The Natural Cycle of External Reinforcement

The additional dimensions that customers are looking for are largely based on education and advice. It is but natural for any customer to look for reinforcement. By not meeting this need consciously, we fail to create a reference anchor in our minds. For example, an entire aggregator and comparison industry has arisen out of this need – hotels, credit cards, loans, electronics, among others. This class of industry players has served to satisfy this need. So much so that a typical journey for the customer looks like this:

1. Visit an aggregator to get a sense of what products and services are available
2. Perform research from multiple sources of aspects other than price and common parameters
3. Decide and buy through the aggregator, or by visiting the underlying provider

We have gotten so used to this model, that improving commerce means fighting this commoditized war through more customer reviews, more discounts, more advertisements, more visibility, and so on. We try to hold on to customers by prompting them for direct purchases the second time, and engage them with various additional discounts through loyalty programs. And it's a spiral we cannot break out of.

But how about focusing on the external reinforcement? That path has largely been ignored. Right from validation of need to validation of choice, we have strong avenues to engage customers in a way that can be unique to us and our value propositions. Every offer is different and has the passion of the team that creates it. But we have reduced that passion to a basic comparison on commoditized parameters. Providing external reinforcement implies we look at the customer need, an outside-in approach. Evaluating the journey that way opens up entirely new avenues of engagement.

For example, a family looking for hotels on their trip to Spain is looking for a reasonably priced hotel, but they are also looking for the best way to make their trip enjoyable – destinations, itineraries, local exploration, gifts to take back, and most of all beautiful memories. How does an aggregator site accomplish that? More importantly should we let them accomplish that? What should our entry point into customer engagement be – the star rating of the hotel, or beautiful memories? Channels to reach customers are important for all of us. That need cannot be ignored. We must be found when customers are looking for us. But what happens then? That's the customer journey that external reinforcement focuses on.

Addition of a New Dimension: The Ecosystem

So far the customer engagement story I have highlighted has brought out two aspects:

1. Linking emotional connections and physical customer interactions
2. Providing external reinforcement

In this section, I'm adding a third critical dimension to this problem of customer engagement. That new dimension is the ecosystem in which we operate. In order to drive customer engagement in a connected world, we also need partnerships with other companies who don't compete with us, but help us address the connected customer journeys in a more complete way. The premise I use is from chapter one. We are all people, not customers. Our needs are interconnected, and the emerging digital world is offering us possibilities to connect these needs. In fact, connecting these diverse needs is a must if we are to compete successfully in the new economy. As soon as companies use this construct, their approach to customer engagement will automatically and dramatically change. What results is then a focus on overall customer engagement and loyalty.

Let's first consider the customer engagement and loyalty efforts in the absence of an ecosystem:

*   Consumer products firms, who are high on the scale of emotional connections and branding, can use tools such as communities, loyalty, experiential programs and DIY

projects to create one-to-one relationships with their customers.

- Hospitality companies are providing connected experiences to their customers through the use of mobile apps that perform various concierge services and utility functions like unlocking rooms or ordering room service. They are providing technology systems that recognize a customer and set the room temperature and lighting accordingly. The end goal is to build travel experiences and get to know local cultures.

- Financial services firms (e.g. Banks) are providing cutting edge services through digital innovation such as voice activated kiosks, retailer promotions, mobile operated ATMs, fast KYC, and real time notifications of transactions.

The evolution above is exciting. Technology is enabling new ways of engaging customers, and enhancing the value of our core products. Quickly, the new capabilities will become a part of the core products.

However, now consider how the above would be done through the power of an ecosystem. A convergence of industries begins to occur:

- Consumer products firms can extend their customer engagement efforts by engaging retailers and service providers who control the physical ends of the spectrum. The power of their customer engagement tools can now be augmented through purposeful physical interactions.

- Hospitality companies can let travelers get in touch with local service providers at the holiday destination. They understood that customers have needs beyond a hotel room at a resort. The end goal is to build travel experiences and get to know local cultures.

- Banks can reinforce their emotional branding established through slogans such as "we focus on your financial future". Every bank says that, but few are really able to get customers to agree. The next evolution for banks is not only to become digital, but to provide financial advice and security. They can only do this through an ecosystem of providers that are on-boarded to keep the customer front and center. The historical purpose of offering retailer promotions was to drive spending on bank cards, which in turn drives up account balances and credit. But in the future, this capability must be supported by building customer 360 that helps with overall financial wellbeing, perhaps through robotic advice on how to manage and invest money. The branches can also be converted to a community hub where experts come together to help customers while serving their own needs, instead of the branch just being a transaction channel. The ecosystem is tightly linked.

The capabilities needed with an ecosystem, are a natural evolution of the capabilities needed without the ecosystem. They build on top of each other. But the new capabilities are dramatically different from the ways we have engaged before. The focus now is squarely on the customer-as-a-person.

So, as is the case with everything in this book, we can now look at customer engagement as an equation:

Customer Engagement

=

[(Interaction + External Reinforcement)

*

(Ecosystem)]

An ecosystem dramatically improves the effectiveness of our customer engagement efforts. We will see how to build ecosystems in the chapter on Integration. For now, let's stay on the topic of customer engagement.

Executing Customer Engagement with an Ecosystem

Going back to the first illustration in this chapter, we saw how the traditional measurements of customer engagement now need to be augmented by ecosystems.

In order to do this, we need to redefine the boundaries of our control. In the current world, we consider our partners to be channels. We cannot for the most part control how they will operate, so we align with their operating model, and try to improve our own metrics to measure to validate our approaches.

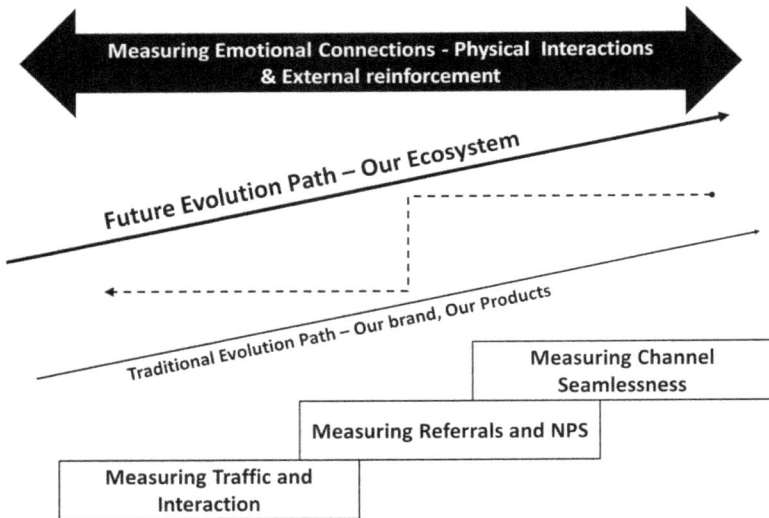

Fig: The New Context of Customer Engagement - Ecosystems

Let's look at the 3 levels briefly. Within each level we will then identify how execution will change when we consider the ecosystem keeping in mind the two levers of:

- Linking emotional connections and physical interactions
- External reinforcement

Level 1: Measuring traffic and interaction

At the first level, it's about measuring the conversions through our own channels and those of our channel partners or aggregators. By measuring the conversions, we can do these things:

1. **Improve our standing** – tactics and strategies such as reviews, landing page designs, product descriptions, photographs, benefits, advertisements, blogs etc.
2. **Understand partner effectiveness** – is this partner worth our investments, or should we look for a new one?
3. **Analyze channel and customer trends** – is this channel itself losing its standing, and are customers moving to other channels?

Traditional digital marketing tactics fall under this category. They are extremely important for improving conversions and awareness.

How does an ecosystem affect this core operating model? In an ecosystem, we are working with partners on next level strategies for mutual benefit, rather than just maximizing what they have to offer us. This means that each player identifies and leverages the competencies that they don't have.

Level 2: Referrals and NPS

At this level, having moved beyond the fundamentals of awareness and conversions, the focus generally shifts to customer satisfaction. This level tries to drive strategic change by analyzing if customers are satisfied enough to refer us to others. Referrals have been considered the holy grail of customer satisfaction. They are also a very reliable measure of whether customers are getting value from our products or services. In addition, the propensity to refer also indicates any external factors beyond value that customers may consider.

It is obvious that the ability to refer appeals significantly to the emotional side of the relationship. Calls to action are also planned around moments when customers are more likely to take action such as after immediately completing a successful transaction.

The NPS (Net Promoter Score) and other popular measures are attempts to understand how customers feel about the relationship (see ref 35). They are actually a combination of many factors distilled into an easy to use score. Think of it like a financial credit score. The number is a good overall indicator of credit worthiness but if we peel back the layers of our credit, we'll discover a lot of insights that may even lead us to question the numeric representation.

Level 3: Measuring Channel Seamlessness

At this level, having moved beyond the fundamentals of awareness, conversions and satisfaction, the focus generally shifts to channel agnostic engagement.

The channels evolution started a decade ago in a multi-channel way. This initial model was all about channel capability. For example, if a promotion was run on the web, it should also be executed in person. And if a customer could take a certain action on the web, that capability should also be provided on mobile. This model brought many benefits and new capabilities and features were added to make all channels capable of performing additional functions as appropriate.

Over time, this model evolved to what we now call as Omni Channel which was a different perspective of looking at multichannel. The idea behind Omni Channel was to look at the channels from a customer perspective. For example, if customers initiated their journey on the phone, then the same conversation was sought to be continued on other channels such as the web or in person. This step has brought tremendous gains for companies, not to mention for the customer.

In addition, innovations are allowing certain channels to experiment with new technologies such as video, artificial intelligence and high level levels of interactivity. A home furnishing provider offering customers the opportunity to see how the furniture looks in their home is an example, as also is a clothing retailer offering customers to see how they look and check inventory is another.

While the Omni Channel journey is still largely incomplete, the world has moved on to better and bigger things. In the rest of this chapter, we'll see how the introduction of ecosystems now presents organizations with a unique opportunity to redefine the boundaries of what Omni Channel has to offer.

Let's use the customer engagement model we defined, and see how our customer engagement is poised to be transformed in this new connected age. In the two strategies below we will look at all three stages of customer experience and engagement:

1. Measuring traffic and interactions
2. Referrals and NPS
3. Channels seamlessness

We will also leverage the concept of connected customer journeys we covered in chapter one.

Linking Emotional Connections and Physical Interactions

By allowing for personalized interactions on our channels that link the value propositions of multiple providers, we can dramatically improve the way we ourselves are presented. This capability requires data sharing and privacy controls, both of which are easily possible today through technology advancements. For example, a traveler that has previously focused on art and history can be shown our offers and amenities at the new destination from that perspective. And a customer that is looking at a mortgage can be shown personalized and tailored impact of their decisions on their financial status.

These capabilities are not just superficial advertising techniques but are based on active and expressed customer interest.

To maintain the ecosystem, interactions will also be bidirectional between any two parties. For example, continuing with our example, customers who end up directly on the hotel's website will probably be shown additional travel advice and planning tools that are provided by their channel partners such as aggregators or local service communities.

Think of what happens. In each of these sample interactions above, the channel partner and product provider take their relationship to a completely new level. They are linking physical interactions with emotional connections by showing how they are living up to their advertised brand promises. In addition, they now operate as one entity with a higher outside-in purpose of helping the customer, thereby making their respective products much more attractive. Keep in mind that use cases can be accomplished through multiple players in an ecosystem. So think of your ecosystem, and proceed accordingly.

Obviously, the way we measure traffic and improve conversions will take on new elements. In addition to explaining traffic patterns and conversion analytics, these measurements will now have strategic inputs into how the capabilities of the ecosystem should evolve. The capabilities we will need will span multiple functional areas such as customer service, product usage experience, sales and marketing.

Now let's look at how customer satisfaction measurement such as NPS can be augmented through this model. An ecosystem presents us with new opportunities to improve this critical metric. Just as it is important to create tangible links between emotional connections and physical interactions within the boundaries of our own organizations, the inclusion of ecosystems takes this to exciting new levels. At the heart of it is the fact that customers are addressing a set of needs that are much beyond our own products and services portfolio. However comprehensively we think we meet our customers' needs, we are but a small element in their overall professional or personal life. And more often than not, what customers do or experience with our products, they take to their interactions with another organization. This is where the opportunity rests to raise the level of customer experience and satisfaction.

Consequently, there are two options. In both options, multiple firms are working together to address the customer experience, and not just their own part of the bargain.

The first option is that the propensity to refer can be created as per an end to end experience, with each NPS separately executed but still offered at key physical interactions that touch their product in some way. For example, a customer that is at a hotel can be asked for a rating for the experience on the channels that got them there. And an aggregator can follow up by asking for how the hotel is performing and how it is living up to the promises it made on the channel. This option links the experiences but keeps the two entities separate. Needless to say, this link between companies will now automatically result in tighter synergy between the customer engagement strategies companies involved. The focus will be on maximizing customer value, not just on their respective products.

The second option is more comprehensive but more difficult to execute. It requires a coherent approach by multiple companies, and hence a commitment to operate as per a packaged experience. Under this option, the entry points into the NPS are merged. The customer is asked about the overall experience of the package. However, the independent satisfaction assessments can still be executed by the participating companies. Let's continue with our travel example. While each provider that participates in the package executes its own interactions, an overall assessment is executed by the party that owns that specific package. Similarly in a scenario that is a partnership between a bank and retail partners, the overall experience measure is captured, in addition to the measurement of individual products by the participating companies. The end result of such an approach is that the value propositions are now focused on the overall customer purpose, rather than on the partial need that each participating company is trying to accomplish.

In both the options above, we can see how the physical interactions are being intricately linked to the emotional connections with customers. The brand promise now extends to focus squarely on customer purpose – what the customer is trying to achieve, rather than what they are going to be using our individual products for. Such an approach takes the NPS or customer satisfaction measurement to match how experiences will be delivered in the future, and what customers will expect in a digital, connected world.

As you can imagine, linking of emotional-physical interactions takes the concept of channel seamlessness to the next level if we consider it in the context ecosystems. An ecosystem approach places the focus squarely on the end to customer experience and forces us to initiate actions that are much more advanced than what we have traditionally done. The concept of a channel has evolved. It is no longer our own channels, but also those of providers whose services and products are linked to ours – both before and after.

The latest innovations in this space that everyone is talking about such as chatbots, voice activated devices such as Apple Siri and Amazon Alexa, video based interaction, are all steps towards creating this new ecosystem. We must think of these as tools to create a connection between physical interactions and emotional connections.

The notion of a channel is not only being expanded but it is being redefined. Everywhere the customers interact with our services is our channel, not someone else's and we need to treat it that way. In addition, we fear that dominance of another company's channel will replace ours in the race for customer engagement, thus rendering us fungible. That fear is valid only if we don't make the interaction 2-way. For example, when Apple Siri pulls our customer's bank balance on Facebook, can we provide customized retailer offers that are unique to our customer's relationship with us. Transactions like these help us live up to the promise our brand is making to our customers. But we must look beyond our own products. For a bank, it's about financial prudence, for a hotel it's about an enjoyable vacation, and for a retailer it's about meeting an aspiration that the product serves to fulfil.

Connecting physical interactions and emotional connections helps us leapfrog commoditization.

Managing External Reinforcement

External reinforcement is a frightening concept. But when we think of acquiring and nurturing the right customers, the notion starts to makes sense. Let's see how customer engagement can be augmented using ecosystems and external reinforcement.

By following up on expressed interests through tangible proof points and advice, we can accomplish the need for external reinforcement. For example, if we know that travelers have expressed an interest in historical sites, can partners collaborate and help customers decide what the best location or itinerary will be. Similarly, customers looking for a large mortgage can be offered assistance in financial planning, or someone looking at a home that needs significant restoration can be guided on that need.

External reinforcement is about helping customers with their need, not just our own products. It has been proven again and again that by being a partner in decision making, we have a higher chance of being the provider of choice as well (see ref 11 and 12).

So a core digital marketing capability such as measuring traffic and conversions will be transformed into a driver for strategic conversations with clients. What do customers want? This question will take on new importance. In addition, measurements will now be provided or exchanged with the participating partners in the ecosystem. All partners will be enabled to review how they engage customers, and how they are helping customers meet their goals. It's a dramatically different understanding and implementation of customer engagement.

Let's see how the capability to provide external reinforcement can affect the customer satisfaction elements. Using the power of the ecosystem for external reinforcement can be very powerful. Consider from the previous section how we used the ecosystem to assess the experience score on an entire package. Using the principle of external reinforcement, we can influence that score at every touchpoint during the package. It makes us more responsive to potentially changing customer needs and providing them with the best option at every stage.

For example, a traveler can encounter changing conditions upon arrival at a destination. Various situations such as weather, holiday, closures, etc. can require them to look at different options to fulfil their intended purpose. An ecosystem approach to their itinerary allows the participating companies to help customers analyze the options that are right for them, instead of leaving the customers to explore these tradeoffs on their own. In fact, by providing the customers with information that is likely to take them away from their original purchases, the ecosystem approach builds trust with the customer that their purpose has not been ignored or forgotten.

Companies may implement tactical retention penalties or win-back mechanisms. However, the fact that the focus is still on the customer's goals will mitigate any customer dissatisfaction with the brand promise. That is because even if the companies do not follow this approach, customers are still likely to explore options on their own. And they will still see the retention or buyback penalties being imposed. In the absence of this external reinforcement in the form of the best options that are available to customers, companies will cede the trusted position to others.

In addition, as soon as customers look for external reinforcement themselves, a break occurs in customer engagement. Instead, we can provide external reinforcement, and make the experiences – purchases – seamless and frictionless to encourage customer decisions in our favor. That engagement is then by choice, and with perfect knowledge that better options are available. Research has shown repeatedly that by creating a reference anchor in our customers' minds, we increase the propensity of them deciding in our favor.

The same model can be extended to any industry. All that is needed, is to think of and build an ecosystem that supports the customer purpose, and hence an end to end customer journey.

Summary

This chapter outlined how we can transform our customer engagement models when we consider ecosystems.

In short, remember this equation if don't anything else.

$$\text{Customer Engagement}$$
$$=$$
$$[(\text{Interaction} + \text{External Reinforcement})$$
$$*$$
$$(\text{Ecosystem})]$$

When we speak of machine learning and artificial intelligence, these techniques can only reach their full potential through the use of ecosystems. That's because these techniques need data and context in order to perform. And rather than trying to piece together data and appearing to be intrusive, we can ask the customers for the data – provided we give them the value.

This new approach also helps us get past the notion of creating value out of the data we collect. We've all heard of how we want to unlock the value of the data through big data analytics and other techniques. Think about it. The mad rush to collect data can be spearheaded more efficiently if we start thinking more proactively about these cross-industry and cross-company experiences first. The analytics can provide new insights which can be put to use, but it's also time to start using big data for what it can do for us – transform customer engagement, rather than making tweaks to it.

In addition, one of the biggest issues we are facing today is of privacy. Why do we have the issue? Is it because we are trying to stay one step ahead of customers without first trying to create a relationship? In cases when my phone tells me that it's a smooth 15 minute ride back home, I feel it's a bitter sweet experience. I'm fascinated, but I'm also a little spooked. What else are they tracking? Similarly, I am frustrated when my favorite retailer and my bank send me completely un-personalized, generic communications to flood my inbox. Then they call me with offers that will never apply to me. I also see my retailer and my bank working together, but it never means anything to me, other than offering up newer discounts and promotions hoping that I'll buy. Like most customers, I have some priorities I am working towards at any point in time – holiday season, upcoming vacation travel, school stuff for my children, new clothes, gifts for family, retirement worries, home upgrade concerns – and so many things. For once, please tell me you want to understand me. I'll be happy to oblige, and engage.

BLOCK 4: INTEGRATION

The connected model of Integration is about how we present ourselves to our customers to build lasting and meaningful customer relationships. It will show us how we need to unify the combined appeal of all our products and services. In addition, this capability will show us how to <u>extend the value of our portfolio by bringing the power of our ecosystem to our customers.</u>

We can think of integration as a way to bring the full power of our products portfolio to our customers. I covered this in a lot of detail in *Dancing The Digital Tune,* and I'll also review that briefly here. For the topic of this book, this subject is even more important when we consider a connected world. To prepare for the future we must create an ecosystem of partners in a new way to extend the value of our portfolio. We'll see in the following pages how that will be extremely important to accomplish so that we can boost customer engagement and interaction.

We've been conditioned to operate in ways that meet our direct goals. And that has resulted in disconnected customer experiences on many fronts. We only have to look at the cross-sell and collaboration efforts at our organizations as examples of those across products, customer engagement and customer service. We tend to present and showcase our offerings by product or business line, and then we tend to structure everything else downstream to align with that approach. In this chapter we'll address how to instead put the customer at the center, and let everything flow from there.

Second, we have been conditioned to treat our partners as service providers, distribution enhancers or portfolio add-ons. We tend to put our product at the center, and then figure out how to market, sell, distribute and retain. We identify distribution channels such as retailers and third party websites, and then we strive to keep our product at the forefront to be visible to customers. However, from a customer centric approach perspective, our efforts leave a lot to be desired. Keeping partners at an arm's length has resulted in metrics that will not work for the emerging connected age. We need to embrace partners and create a fabric of seamless customer engagement with them. In this chapter, we'll discuss the framework and approaches to do just that.

Third, in a connected ecosystem, we need to build a heart. What do we stand for and how we identify with customers? These topics have been the foundations of branding strategy and in a connected world, these questions ring true in a very dramatic fashion. When seamless payments and automatic transactions through our watches, refrigerators, phones, home entertainment systems, and even washing machines will make it difficult to get ahead of when the transaction originates, how will we establish a preference for us? I'm sure it won't be through more coupons and discounts because there won't be anything different in what we do. The solution will be to un-commoditize, to connect with customers on causes that they care strongly about, and to create an ecosystem of partners through which we can focus on meeting the customers' overall goals.

As we embark on creating an ecosystem, generally speaking, the following high level benefits framework can apply as a preliminary evaluation of the nature of partnerships:

Customers:

1. Meet and manage end goals
2. Increase convenience
3. Garner financial incentives

Ecosystem of Businesses:

1. Address connected customer journeys
2. Retention due to intermingled services
3. More frequent engagement
4. New customers
5. Emotional connections
6. Multiple (multi-business) entry points into the customer engagement spectrum

The framework provides an effective way to quickly evaluate partnerships we must establish.

The Integration Model

The model is simple, and I'll depict it with the graphic below, and also review some preliminary material from *Dancing The Digital Tune*:

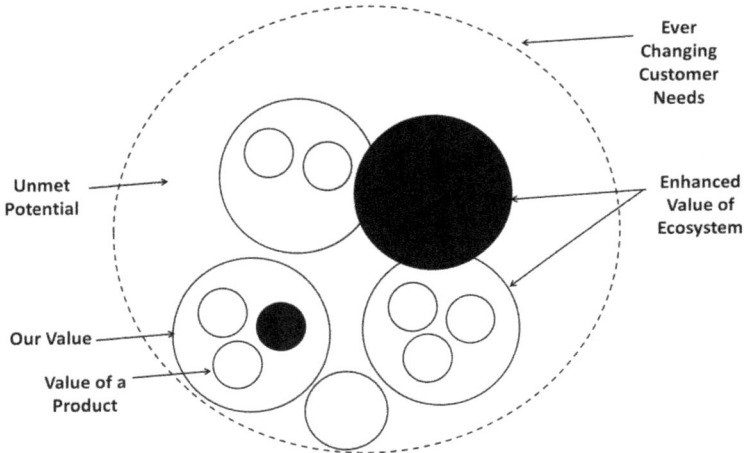

Fig: Integrating to enhance the power of our portfolio

Read the illustration like this:

Sum of our products

+

Sum of our ecosystem

+

Unmet potential

=

Customer needs

When a firm sells an individual product, it is meeting a portion of the customer's need. And over time, a firm advances into adjacent areas to slowly meet broader customer needs or to attract different types of customers.

- A razor manufacturer makes disposable razors and electric razors, and then begins to make shaving gels as well as after shave products
- A bank begins to offer retirement planning services and wealth management services
- A software products company begins to make software in newer areas or provides professional services
- And so on

Businesses start out narrow and then expand. Amazon started as an online book-seller. Banks started by offering savings accounts. Google started as a search company. Microsoft started as an operating system. Many Indian software services companies started with economical and quality offshore IT project delivery. Unilever and P&G likely started with soap or cream. Nike probably started with shoes. In some cases, companies assume new identities as markets change and their original brand no longer covers their new line. 3M, LG are some examples of companies that overhauled their identities. More often than not, the product line extensions and expansions are linked by a common, underlying customer need. That customer need is often also the organization's core purpose and vision as set by the founders.

The first aspect of integration in the equation above (sum of our products), is about unifying the appeal of our products and services to facilitate seamless interaction. It is about reducing the friction between our product offerings. We have a problem if our business operates in silos, and makes the customer jump through hoops to understand and buy our products. Our business must look and behave with a single minded focus on the customer.

The concept of integration we are addressing in this chapter goes beyond linking our own products together. From the illustration before and from the second part of the equation above (sum of our ecosystem), the spectrum of customer needs far exceeds what one organization can offer. This premise was also the basis of the connected customer journeys we discussed in chapter one. Consumers evaluate and buy products that meet various needs. What this means is that we must move on from joint ventures and partnerships that serve to satisfy the narrow need that our product offerings were intended to serve. Instead we must move to begin to treat our customers in light of their overall needs and aspirations. Traditionally, the focus has been on partners that help us accomplish our core functions better, cheaper and faster. In essence we establish partnerships with the inside-out approach – looking at customers from our own vantage point. However, going forward, ecosystems of companies will drive this partnerships model. The ecosystems will address the wholeness of a customer's identity, not just a specific need that our business seeks to satisfy. It follows that businesses that have nothing to do with the value chain of our own business will be strong candidates for partnerships.

These futuristic examples illustrate this point:

- Where health and fitness centers had little connection to retail, they now often partner with health food manufacturers and retailers to develop joint programs to boost customer engagement and meet a need of the customer pursuing a healthy lifestyle. All three parties benefit by working together.

- Where banks participate in the fitness and health arena by creating mechanisms for customers to pursue healthy habits in return for better banking benefits.
- Where credit card companies that monitor spending and balances on their cards, would co-brand with not one, but multiple service providers and retailers to launch a multi-branded offering. All parties are now facilitators of customer needs based on overall spending patterns and wish lists.

A customer centric view implies that we must look at our organization outside-in through our customers' eyes.

- When and where are they looking to fit in our product category?
- What products are they fitting in and in which places that don't concern our products?
- When they don't fit in with our product, what other products are they consuming?

The entire digital revolution that has laid traditional business obsolete is based on this principle. There is still a long way to go for the focus to shift to the customer needs. Today, we are still only taking advantage of the technology capabilities to upgrade existing business models. It's a significant jump, but only an incremental one when viewed from the vantage point of the Principle of Completion.

- Amazon has expanded from being simply an online bookseller to a rapidly growing marketplace. It has adjusted its core service into the needs spectrum of the online world. It could have been satisfied by simply being an online store for books and music. But Amazon used its paid shipping model (Prime membership) and its marketplace to engage with changing customer behavior from music to movies to Kindle to everything under the sun. The focus is still on Amazon though, not on the industry ecosystem.

- Starbucks has effectively used its mobile application to accept payments from customers. Previously, Starbucks utilized a third party network, but with the new app it is now driving more traffic, more engagement, more promotions and more loyalty. And if it expands its payment mechanisms to help other retailers, does Starbucks have a shot at being at the center of a shopping revolution?

- Target has used its REDcard to reduce the cost of doing business while improving personalization and loyalty. The 5% discount is tough for most people to pass up. It remains to be seen how the REDcard will progress beyond Target to encompass the other networks that its customers leverage to meet their needs.

While interesting and often talked about, the successes so far are only the tip of the iceberg. The digital world offers such a huge potential, and most of it is still untapped.

To put this in perspective, let's review what I call the social face of a company.

Our Social Face

"Nobody ever saw a dog make a fair and deliberate exchange of one bone for another with another dog. Nobody ever saw one animal by its gestures and natural cries signify to another, this is mine, that yours; I am willing to give this for that....But man has almost constant occasion for the help of his brethren, and it is in vain for him to expect it from their benevolence only – Adam Smith, The Wealth of Nations

For a moment, consider our customers to be the "architects of their dreams". And then think how we could be a partner in their efforts to realize their goals and passions?

It's actually a question of survival that doesn't leave much choice. We must evolve from being an enabler of transactions and a provider of products to being a partner that helps customers achieve their dreams. We are at an inflection point. As consumer interactions and behavior become more connected across industries, and across channels, it is extremely important for us to continue evolving our view of the consumers and embed ourselves deeper into the entire experience cycle.

How should we define a face of our organizations that will expand the boundaries of relationship management and customer engagement? This question implies that we understand and act upon customer and partner perspectives throughout their experience lifecycle and life-stages, taking into consideration both direct and indirect customers. Effective development of this position can directly drive key parameters such as acquisitions, account growth, cross sell and retention. Think of this position as an ecosystem we orchestrate. For our purposes, this ecosystem will not be defined as a group characterized by sharing of common values or even collaborating with or helping each other. To do that would be to limit it to a partial dimension. Instead, this ecosystem is a coming together of people with different motivations, who help each other by striving to meet their own needs. The structure of what we do with the ecosystem defines the context of what it is. In this context, an ecosystem community is a coming together of consumers and various service providers (commercial or charity) to satisfy mutual needs. This is how connected customer journeys will come to life.

It is important to note that most organizations have not one target segment but many. Indeed, the product, marketing and service models are as many as required to serve and satisfy these segments. An ecosystem will allow customers to truly interact and engage across their needs spectrum, because it is focused on them, not on the products.

The social face (or the ecosystem) is characterized by:

- Minimizing external reinforcement which implies that customers can find an anchor or reference point that helps them select what's best for them in full context of what their need is
- Providing multiple entry points into the ecosystem by encouraging the users (consumers, customers and partners / merchants) to promote the ecosystem as a destination for needs definition and solution analysis
- Allowing all participants to have a targeted, personalized experience backed by the power of local community connect

In its simplest form – along an ecosystem maturity curve - the "Social Face" of the bank can be viewed as a combination of socially integrated web and mobile toolkits that bring together the most common activities of the consumer. Personalization and targeting in the community will be brought about by segmentation based on type (e.g. commercial, personal) and level (e.g. premium) aided by social, regional and demographic intelligence. And most importantly the personalization will be one-one eliminating the need for guesswork. Predictive analytics will have its place but only as a means to enhance this interaction.

Customer groups within this ecosystem can also be considered as communities. Different segments will make up the community. For example one segment may access their social causes and campaigns at both local and national levels, another may meet as a group and benchmark their upcoming travel and holiday purchases, while a third segment may monitor their social networks while reviewing their accounts to plan and review their financial goals for education or retirement.

Going beyond industry boundaries, such an ecosystem brings together parties like health and fitness providers, non-profits, professional or family organizations and connects them through an appropriate fitment of their product offerings and transactional needs.

- First, the partnership, which is based on the customers' trust for advice will be enhanced through the arrangement of offerings around customers' needs, backed by the views and opinions of the community itself. In other words, the aim of eliminating external reinforcement – the most deadly cause for loss of customer engagement today – will be fulfilled.

- Second, switching costs, one of the primary methods to increase retention will rise a notch above those of the common tools in use today. The premise is that as customers independently work off checklists, loyalty programs, shopping lists, social campaigns, ROI computations, wish-lists, and future plans within the ecosystem, there is an increased affinity to the ecosystem because the focus on customer needs allows the community to address multiple aspects of a transaction in a personalized and contextual manner, An ecosystem does have natural switching costs. But it will not consciously inhibit voluntary movement out of the ecosystem into a competing ecosystem. True customer partnership implies that we are willing to let go. And even though it seems contradictory, informed self-selection often promotes growth and profitability (see ref 11 and 12). That's what branding and positioning is all about – focus.

- Third, a self-sustaining ecosystem will gradually be built as both individuals and participating business entities (such as banks, insurers, hotels, local providers, airlines, retailers, charities etc.) in the ecosystem try to maximize their own returns. These are through the 3-Tier Loyalty models we have discussed in the previous chapters.

These are but a few of the characteristics of ecosystem development which focus on the goal of putting yourself at the forefront of the channel war, addressing the full spectrum of use cases and needs through a partner ecosystem thus minimizing the threat of being relegated as a commodity service provider. Customers may of course be part of more than one ecosystem as partners will compete, but the share of wallet will go to the ecosystem that wins by keeping the user's (customers, consumers and partners) needs in the forefront while constantly aligning and positioning their offerings to both expressed as well as latent needs discovered through the community interaction.

This is how platforms will become apps within larger platforms. Put another way, once you're in, you're family.

Let's now discuss the mechanics of creating such an ecosystem.

- **Identify the ecosystem:** Who should we partner with and include in our ecosystem?
- **Balance corporate priorities**: How should we create a model where priorities of the partners are inherently at conflict with each other?

As I've reiterated throughout this book, the foundation of defining the right ecosystem is to look at our customers as people, not as buyers of our products and services. The needs of our customers are much broader than what we sell. And their aspirations and motivations cover much larger ground than our own sales and marketing activities. A lot of research has been done already on brand alliances as well as strategic alliances. Identifying the ecosystem relies on those fundamentals but expands the concept to be truly customer purpose driven.

In other words, we will put the customer at the center.

The concept of creating an ecosystem instead of a partnership is based on our discussion of connected customer journeys from chapter one. In those customer journeys, we expanded the touch-points to those beyond our own organization. In *Dancing The Digital Tune*, I discussed the concept of a chain of links. The premise behind that was simple. Even though the traditional business world is segregated by industries, products and domains, the truth is that today's customer experience is increasingly cross-industry. It's not that customers have inherently changed, but it's because new possibilities are now being discovered through emerging technology capabilities.

So when we identify the ecosystem as per the connected customer journeys, we must think of 2 things:

1. **Connected Customer Journeys**

    A connected customer journey indicates the right partners to include in our ecosystem. We might start with a small part of the connected customer journey and over time expand to cover more. Or we might be only able to develop a limited type of connected customer journey which we implement before new possibilities come to light.

    For example, supermarkets may start with an ecosystem that only includes certain fitness centers. Customers can be nurtured jointly towards a comprehensive plan that helps the customer towards their fitness goals. The supermarket can create a well-defined and predictable pipeline of orders, while the fitness center can secure higher retention of customers. Both these participants can then bring in additional players such as dieticians, the local cultural, and sporting groups etc. The ecosystem is limited only by imagination.

The important thing to remember is that this ecosystem is very different from a blind approach to customer engagement that relied on advertising and mass marketing. An ecosystem follows an outside-in approach and is focused on overall customer purpose in two ways. First, the ecosystem allows for the participants to engage in a personalized manner with the customers because it knows what the customer's goals are, rather than guessing them. Second the ecosystem allows every participant to take input from other participants. This mutual relationship means that each participant focuses on maximizing customer value. If it doesn't do that, then its value in the ecosystem diminishes automatically.

2. **Risk**

Any partnership has risk. However, the ecosystem model has a very specific risk – that of losing control of the customer experience. Once that happens, the product that is not in front of the customer can be commoditized. There are several ways to mitigate this risk. First, the partnership must be explicitly 2-way which means that an ecosystem partnership is not just about being a distribution, supply or channel partner. Instead, all parties in the ecosystem must jointly own the customer front end and be able to reinforce end-to-end customer journey. For this reason, the various aggregator models are not ecosystem partnerships. The second way to mitigate this risk is to establish barriers or incentives that keep access to the customer experience open. For examples, banking or other services accessed through the chat or voice services of other companies may adopt this approach to combat commoditization.

As you can imagine, partnerships and ecosystems work best when both sides of the partnership do their part to together create a customer journey that delights the customer – education, price, service.

However, the partnerships above are meant to be multi-dimensional. Both partners have products or services and they work together to create an alliance that helps them both. The most successful partnerships are those where both partners actively keep the goal of the partnership at the forefront of their operating model.

There are 3 major differences from a strategic alliance:

1. First, this arrangement can be, but should not be limited to being just a strategic alliance or partnership. A strategic alliance has formal commitments to each other. And there are generally exclusivity clauses. The ecosystem partnership is where the customer experience is loosely opened up, but full control still remains with each participant.
2. Second, the value of a partner is controlled by the value they are able to deliver to the other participants in the ecosystem. There is hence an automatic checks and balance.
3. The integration of the participants and what binds them to the ecosystem is driven by data sharing to drive the appropriate customer experiences. And the open nature of this data sharing may allow other participants to join as needed. This means that the partnerships are more fleeting than one would imagine. Partnerships that add value will remain, and those that fail will automatically exit the ecosystem.

Let's take a simple example to illustrate this point. A supermarket and a fitness center may strike up an alliance. They establish a model where the fitness center shares standardized diet plans with the supermarket. It also presents the supermarket as a potential avenue to buy food. In return, the supermarket, through the use of a common identifier, and based on the customers' consent, could share the customers' purchases with the fitness center. This closes the loop with the customer who now has access to assistance from both parties to keep them on track to meet their fitness goals. Other companies could enter the ecosystem and offer additional value to the customers.

Over time, this ecosystem will become a strong driver of customer engagement, and will also build up various kinds of retention incentives to customers. As we progress, each of these players can be part of multiple such ecosystems depending on where their customers are. Innovation at each of companies will be on 2 levels – core product or service innovation, and innovation to add additional value to the ecosystem. The priorities for each may be sales influence, service differentiation, or price advantages. The composition of the ecosystem will change depending on various scenarios as partners assess the value they are providing in return for their investments. This is not unlike a regular marketplace. One partner may dominate the equation, another may only provide commoditized services, or a partner may provide more investments in one ecosystem and ignore the other. Players will operate in multiple ecosystems and together address the end to end customer journeys.

Summary

This chapter on integration brought out how we can begin to address the end to end customer journey. We began with the concept of a social face which was a representation of how multiple players can come together and interact contextually with the customers. By working towards their own goals but leveraging data and capabilities from each other with customer consent, each player multiplies the outcomes in customer engagement. In the marketplace, innovations occurring everyday indicate how the conversation is already changing from bringing our own products together to being part of a larger ecosystem. Being focused on customer purpose is contributing to this evolution. Changing customer expectations on their experiences are a big part of this change too. Customers expect our interactions with them to be highly contextual. As we have seen, extended customer personas cannot be met without connecting with others.

The art of bringing our own products together has not been learnt yet. And yet, now the dialog is expanding to include connections with other companies. In this chapter we saw how our value is magnified through such an effort. We also discussed tactics and strategies to embark on this journey.

BLOCK 5: EXECUTION

::

The Execution capability will perhaps clarify the biggest challenge facing leaders today – how to execute and thrive in a new connected world. This chapter combines various techniques and outlines practical methods to get going and build on the momentum. We will explore the concept of creating CX focused communities, what CX focused organizational design looks like, and how the traditional concept of the balanced scorecard model should be adapted to turn our companies into connected powerhouses.

There is an interesting research study (see ref 7) *that* shows that being customer centric can actually decrease financial performance by almost 23%. This research definitely got my attention. Especially in an age where everyone is singing how wonderful customer centricity is.

As I dug deeper, I found that the study brought out 3 key aspects:

1. First, customer satisfaction positively increased due to better and more focused attention by firms on their customers
2. Financial performance increased by 8% in cases where competitive activity was weak, and where competitors were not already customer centric
3. Financial performance degraded by 23% where competitors were already customer centric and where competition was strong

The first result was sort of expected. But result 3 above was surprising. Apparently, there were 2 core drivers of the above results. First, organizational overhead or coordination increased significantly in a customer centric organization. This wasn't too much of a surprise. Second, in cases where there were high levels of competitive activity, very little was typically gained by way of uncovering innovative approaches and meeting unaddressed customer needs. Given that being customer centric is actually supposed to drive this very result, the study brought out a very interesting anomaly.

There is no arguing with data. Ready to abandon being customer centric? Not quite because I do have good news for you.

Here goes.

1. First, how customer centric you are probably cannot be determined solely by top level organizational structures and business divisions. Empirical data is always collected "after" such studies bring out these dramatic revelations. The catch-22 is that existing data does not always tell the whole story.
2. Second, even in an organization structured by customer segments, there is lots of coordination and alignment of

incentives against a largely standard product portfolio that doesn't actually change much by customer segment. The results of the study may have been skewed by this fact. Many organizations hence are never really customer centric to begin with. They are just organized like that.

3. Finally, organizations may indeed have specific and tailored product offerings aligned by customer segments. The claims of being ineffective in a strong competitive field are true only if we factor in the dominance of uniform and similar offerings from one organization to the next. Such product portfolios hence are commoditized competing on price and inertia.

Clearly the right kind of innovation and how we meet customer needs is a critical factor. Brand plays an important role in being distinctive and preferred but it must be supported by the underlying differentiated value propositions. The much needed innovation to evolve our ecosystems is often overlooked in customer centric story lines.

Moreover, the digital and connected world is presenting us with even new and unaddressed challenges. No longer is it about our products alone, but about how we are able to create an ecosystem to meet customer needs. A central premise of this book is that the world is getting connected across industry boundaries. Hence our traditional go-to-market by product lines is slowly being rendered inadequate. Instead, we need to define our go-to-market by cross-industry customer experiences. These experiences in turn must be defined by the overall purpose of our customers. Consequently, that focus on the customer's purpose will extend beyond our products alone.

Everywhere we look, and as outlined in this book, the market is evolving slowly towards this new model. But many of us are still looking inside-out, not outside-in. Hence our customer centric structures don't yield results.

So what can we do to meet this challenge of being customer centric? It's a fact of life that everything evolves. And what are considered as traditional approaches do not always work well in the future. That's not a new phenomenon or claim that I'm making. We evolve, and we always resist new things. That's why we have innovators, early adopters, and even laggards. This is true for management and leadership as well. Some might draw an analogy with a frog in boiling water: if the water heats up slowly the frog won't jump out until it is too late. We've seen that with many companies in the past decade and many more are expected in the future.

So the question we need to address is: how should we change to improve our chances of not only surviving, but also thriving?

There are many possible approaches, and I'm basing this chapter about execution capability on three pillars. We'll look at the rationale for all three, why they make sense, and how to execute on the connected promise.

These are new names but not for old things. They are new names for updated things so we don't get hung up with the preconceptions of the past. Often times the ideal solution for this evolution starts from the top. But as we'll see in this chapter, when the top fails to do what they are supposed to do, there are things we can do from the bottom to help them along. Remember, after all is said and done, we are really solving for people to be successful, and aligning our success, and theirs, to the corporate goals. Let me summarize the three pillars so you know what's coming:

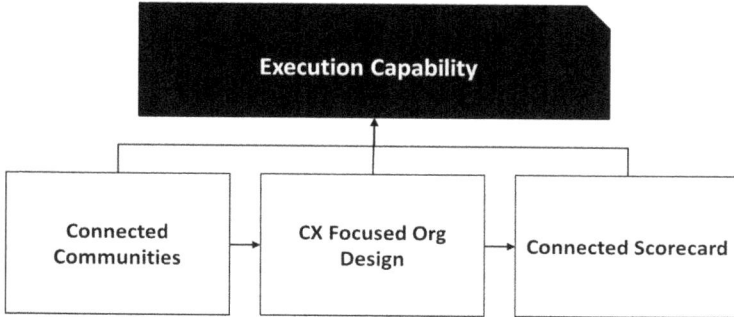

Fig: 3 Pillars of the Execution Capability

Connected Communities

To meet the challenge of how product innovation itself is being redefined in a connected world, we'll look at communities with a twist. We all know about communities and have tried them in various forms and shapes in our organizations. These are basically collections of people who have grouped themselves by the areas they are most interested in, and have been provided tools to collaborate and do stuff. However, more often than not, the collaboration portals are deserted, chat forums are listless, and there are spikes of activities every now and then when someone feels they need to do something about the area they are passionate about. So, in this chapter we'll look at providing them with a purpose, so we can allow them to make a real impact.

CX Focused Org Design

We are all customer centric. Or at least we claim to be. We put the customer at the center of everything we do. But then, we turnaround and divide our organization by products, and businesses, and geographies. Then we valiantly strive to realize the power of all our capabilities to serve the customer through layers of integration and coordination. Obviously, this approach is missing an essential ingredient that causes to fall short of realizing the full potential. In *Dancing The Digital Tune*, I had outlined a reverse pyramid. We'll build on that given our focus on a connected ecosystem. We'll define how to create a CX focused org design.

Connected Scorecard

This scorecard brings everything together. We all know about the Balanced Scorecard (see ref 9). I've updated the classic Balanced Scorecard model to give us a new practical framework for driving, and measuring, our effectiveness in a connected world. People and how they are motivated along the desired path are critical for a good org design. No amount of coaxing can accomplish what we don't or can't measure. So this section will highlight how everything will come together to create a CX focused org powerhouse.

Ready for take-off? Here we go!

Connected Communities

If there is one challenge in the corporate world that still needs attention, it's that of breakthrough innovation. We've heard tens of theories about how to make it work but time and again, the only truly successful stories are those where the agenda has been driven from the top. And even then, the causes of organizational inertia have caused most efforts to fail (see ref 37) with successful ones being created as a result of a separate autonomous business unit.

And now, breakthrough innovation is even more challenging because of the connected nature of products. As customer interaction patterns and channels change, will our product lines, however innovative, be able to maintain the same affinity with customers they did before?

In fact, business innovation today is more than about core products and business alone. The connected nature of businesses can render an innovative product obsolete rapidly. In this section, we'll look at how the traditional concept of innovation itself has gained many additional dimensions.

- Only a few years ago, wearable devices were all the rage. But in the span of a few short years, they are struggling to develop longer lasting affinity with customer usage (see ref 38).
- Our favorite manufacturers of our favorite everyday products are under tremendous pressure because of the organic and natural trend. So many new brands have cropped up. In fact, direct online ordering through machines or connected devices is a threat to established channels and

their understanding of customer behavior (see ref 40). And the change in public sentiment on health is causing them to look at the food labels more than they look at the brand (see ref 40)

What I'm getting at is that any innovation today has to be examined in terms of the ecosystem that is emerging or likely to emerge around a business process. We have to look beyond our products and their customers. And therefore the concept of innovation takes on a new meaning.

In the new connected model ecosystems are underlying everything we will do. Hence, innovation needs to be approached differently from how we have debated it before. This comes from two important observations:

First, as the concept of Innovators Dilemma (see ref 32) logically argues, it is very difficult for businesses to pivot when the core sources of revenue are at stake. A strong recommendation provided by the author is the idea of creating the innovation as a separate autonomous business unit. But this argument only holds when there are traditional models that are not immediately at risk, but new disruptive competition is on the horizon to which they must respond – the actions that must be taken when the industry is about to take on a new dynamic, and when our current business must meet the challenge or perish? For example, when Amazon launched their online business, the response by incumbents should have been to compete head-to-head but they didn't because the core business inertia stopped them from doing so. A similar case exists when new business models launched in the form of Airbnb, Uber, Lyft and Netflix. However consider the competition between Amazon and

Netflix, and the traditional comparison doesn't hold. The innovation is not narrowly disruptive or starting in a niche. It's a steady battle for expansion where I believe amazon has an inherent advantage because it is building up an array of offers all knit together by its Prime program while gradually also building up the value of individual product lines (video streaming in this case). But it'll be an interesting battle to witness because ultimately it will be about who has a stronger ecosystem. We see a similar issue today with consumer brand organizations unable to keep up with new ways of customer ordering patterns such as through mobile apps that make your shopping list, or the Amazon Dash button (see ref 40).

Second, the building up of new innovative products and businesses is not a sustainable model in the age of digital and connected. This is because the power of an ecosystem can far more effectively meet customer needs. As customers become increasingly connected, the entry points to the customers become more numerous. For example, a banking or insurance product is hidden behind voice activated devices run by our favorite technology companies (Apple, Google, Amazon). These companies are aiming to take over the customer front end and relegate the underlying products to little more than fungible commodities. It is imperative for product companies to think beyond distribution channels and consider how they can create customer experiences that span multiple businesses across multiple industries. That doesn't come easily to businesses that have to deliver results on a day to day basis, or which are trying to launch a new innovation as a product or business.

Other models have been proposed to address these challenges with innovation. A well-known example is that of ambidextrous organizations (see ref 8) which has its merits but suffers from some of the same drawbacks when it comes to a connected business world. In my opinion, it is more suited for new products or innovations rather than connecting products and industries to create new value propositions. In the book Accelerate! (see ref 36), the author presents the concept of volunteer based, self-driven passionate communities that are given a purpose and allowed to innovate under the auspices of top management. These communities look for quick wins and slowly begin to integrate the innovation with the core business operations. The reason they fall outside the core business operations is because the priorities of the business are at odds with the long term goals for obvious reasons. The communities are created in alignment with emerging strategic priorities, initially populated by invitation, grown through self-selection, and provided assistance to make many small incremental innovations that then become main-stream in business operations, thus eventually evolving the fundamental nature of operations. This approach fills an important gap in the way communities are managed and nurtured today where their actions have little linkage to the strategic priorities of the business. Lack of linkage with strategic priorities has resulted in communities becoming knowledge sharing and training grounds but are unable to impact the actual business in any substantial manner.

So the concept of innovation I recommend has to be about spanning connected customer experiences across industry and product lines. Setting the innovations up a separate business unit is not going to cut it because the way to play is not individualistic. The "connected communities" as I call them are almost like industry consortiums but only much broader –

operating across industries. In fact, these communities span partners from multiple industries to bring the purpose of customers to life.

My premise is that the design to achieve our customer centric efforts must be created consciously with a focus on customer purpose. Connected Communities must evolve the customer interactions of existing products. At the same they must also be disjointed from a singular focus on our own product portfolio to avoid the innovators dilemma. The efforts cannot be separate business units because of two reasons:

1. The effort needs to expand the value proposition of current products as per an ecosystem. So it needs sponsorship from current business. The last thing we need is conflicting management metrics leading to resistance and in-fighting (e.g. channel usage, channel contributions etc.). Humans are very good at this game.
2. Separate business units need a formal charter which is not often available at early stages of a changing market. We should avoid situations where measurements are created as per metrics that do not move the business forward (e.g. double counting or transferring revenue).

Instead, these new connected communities have a simpler charter - to span connected customer experiences. They need to operate much like an industry consortium and cut across industry and product lines. The communities include partners from multiple industries to bring cross-company customer journeys to life. And then, looking outside in, create and pilot new CX programs within their organizations to stitch various product portfolios together.

The key message is to create and gain momentum on a CX program from the outside in, and then use it to enhance and evolve the core, cash cow operations. Google's famous 20% policy was an informal policy that is now evolving towards a formal innovation model. Citi's Fintech initiative is an example which aligns more with ambidextrous model with a more formal construct. Both of these models have their merits, but they are still not meeting the needs of the future connected world.

A model that is closer to what a connected community will deliver is perhaps the partnership of Wells Fargo with Intuit. Intuit customers are small businesses which need a seamless way to access their bank accounts for accounting purposes. Wells Fargo is providing the API to accomplish this. Another nice model we have seen before is the partnership between Blue Cross Blue Shield and Lifetime Fitness. It's about connecting cross industry and cross company value propositions. These models have been offered to customers for a long time but are now being offered consciously influence customer engagement strategies. This innovation is CX focused and closely links the customer experiences of both firms. While both of these are nice innovations, they still have a long way to go to tackle the ecosystem challenges that await them.

The Connected Community concept can be represented as:

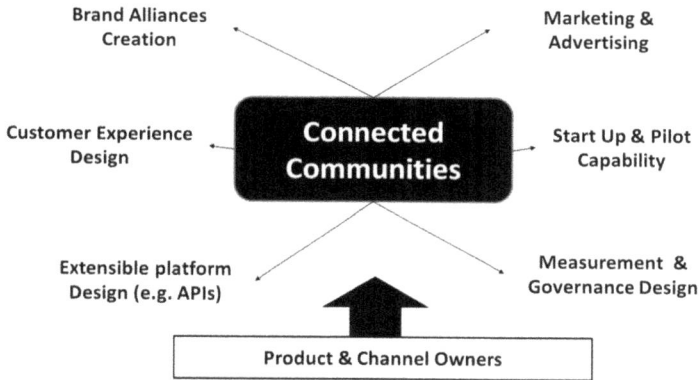

Fig: Conceptual Composition of Connected Communities

As we can see the responsibilities of connected communities span across the entire lifecycle. These include incubating brand alliances which will evolve to being full scale operational and customer engagement partners. This is done through creating the desired customer experience and journeys, thinking of technology extensibility, all the way to executing pilot programs, and marketing.

The connected communities can be called by any name. The important thing to remember is that they are not tied to current operations, but still are working with the sponsorship of the key product and business owners.

The next big hurdle is to operationalize these CX programs. The section on CX Focused Org design explains this.

CX Focused Org Design

Surprisingly, the topic of whether being customer centric makes sense or not has been the subject of much debate in recent years. Various research studies have been conducted and some show how being customer centric actually may decrease profitability and increase costs.

As I mentioned earlier in this chapter, a research of Fortune 500 firms showed that firms operating in markets with strong competitive activity where competitors were already customer centric, exhibited a 23% lower financial performance (see ref 7). And where the competitive activity was weak or where competitors were not already customer centric, the performance increased by 8%. According to the study, these strange results stem from the fact that internal costs of coordination often exceed the financial benefits of being customer centric. Additionally, in cases where competitors are already mature, fewer additional customer needs are to be discovered, and although customer satisfaction increases, the financial results are not commensurate.

However, before we draw any specific conclusions for ourselves, we should note that such research is conducted on available data which is by definition limited – if they knew such research will be conducted, organizations would have collected more data on contributing costs and benefits. While the studies do bring out an awareness of the many pitfalls that should be considered, they do not shed light on other important parameters. For example, we often review highest level organization structures because data is easily available.

With this background, let's understand how we can prepare and design our organizations to be ready for a connected world. The premise of this book is that independent platforms of today will start to interact with each other to maintain relevance. Those are the requirements of an increasingly connected world. In essence, we can consider these platforms as apps within a broader interconnected platform. The independent platforms cannot hope to function in isolation and thrive. And hence, designing for the future is about thinking very clearly about customer experiences in an ecosystem, not customer experiences in an independent corporate context.

That is why when we think of a CX focused org design, we must move beyond the organizational boundaries of business units and product lines. The very definition of what is means to be customer centric changes dramatically. Although traditional constructs of products and business lines are needed to drive order and accountability, they are not enough as we move forward. And it is exactly because of this that existing research falls short. Let's compare a couple of models:

- Organizations are structured by product lines or brands, and directly go to market. There may be internal shared services or none at all.
- Organizations include a customer centric layer that now funnels all brands. Essentially, the customers are managed and approached by a singular entity.

In both the above models, the formal hierarchy may include business units or customer segments for financial reporting purposes. However, as we'll find out, this fact is actually irrelevant for operations.

To understand more easily, some illustrations of these models are below. For simplicity, not all details are shown of course.

Model 1 is the traditional model and many companies still approach customers this way. Strong customer facing brands within a company (e.g. within the Consumer Packaged Goods sector) tend to follow this model.

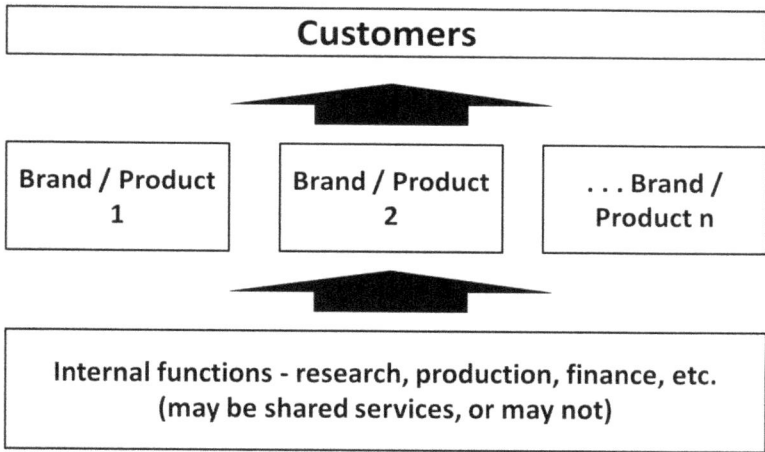

Fig: Model 1 of Org Design

Model 2 is followed more broadly by relationship oriented firms (e.g. B2B technology) or those where individual products are too diverse (e.g. retail, or CPG to Retail).

I did not include a customer segment dimension here because although important, that distinction is superfluous and brands / products already account for that distinction. For example, organizations may have sectoral (retail, financial services, oil & gas, services, travel etc.) and geographic (Europe, North

America, Benelux etc.) divisions, and may also create multiple sub-divisions within these top level divisions.

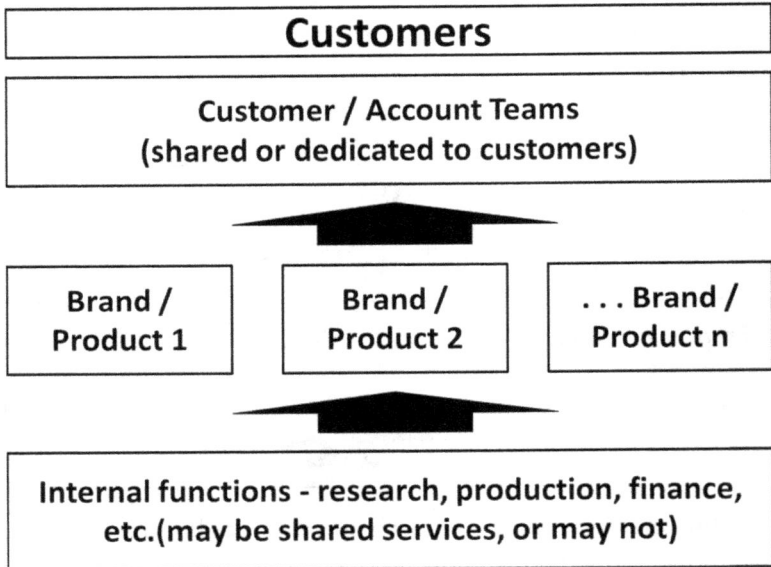

```
+--------------------------------------------------+
|                  Customers                       |
+--------------------------------------------------+
|          Customer / Account Teams                |
|      (shared or dedicated to customers)          |
+--------------------------------------------------+
```

| Brand / Product 1 | Brand / Product 2 | . . . Brand / Product n |

```
+--------------------------------------------------+
| Internal functions - research, production,       |
| finance, etc.(may be shared services, or may not)|
+--------------------------------------------------+
```

Fig: Model 2 of Org Design

In Model 2, you will notice a customer or account team. This structure arguably enables us to bring together customer needs through a single funnel into the organization. This model is effective in situations where many different products are relevant to a single customer through multiple products, and the total value provided to the customers will be enhanced through this integrated go-to-market approach. Model 2 also allows us to identify new areas of opportunity more easily thus driving both innovation as well as expanded customer interaction.

Every organization looks at external trends and evolving trends. However, both model 1 and model 2 are based on an inside-out approach. They identify innovation and then apply it to their products. However, the internal divisions to be integrated are often engaged in a tug of war with the individual products and brands, with each division having to deliver results that are disjointed from the others. We'll cover this specific aspect in the next section on connected scorecards.

As we understand what a CX focused organizational design looks like, and how it complements customer centricity, let's revisit a core principle again:

Industry boundaries are crumbling. Traditional models are based on how we go to market as a company. The new models will be based on how we go to market by customer experiences. And customer experiences in turn must be defined outside-in by customer purpose.

And here's the big scoop:

The top level structure of the company should be driven by interconnected CX programs. Everything else including products and channels should fall under these programs. A CX program is one that is focused on the purpose of customers, not the company's financial goals.

Let's spend a few minutes understanding this so we can start thinking about operationalizing it. In recent years, every new innovation that has taken the industry by storm has altered the traditional definition of customer experience of that industry. And sometimes, it has taken several years before competitors have followed. Nike's focus on health and fitness caused it to approach consumers with a completely new value proposition that was over and above that of offering something lighter and stronger. The individual value propositions took a back seat to experiences which included a network of customers and a variety of local, community based organizations. Of late, Under Armour has made tremendous progress almost following a similar model, although with a branding twist that features underdogs in addition to super stars. Similarly, Amazon's rise was based on creating an ecosystem and an overarching program (Amazon Prime) into which every offer is integrated. Airbnb, Lyft and Uber are known as tech companies, but the driving force for growth is how they focused on a new experience that was lacking, and did not meet customer needs in a connected world. In financial services, early innovators such as Betterment and FutureAdvisor created a new market but are being met head on by incumbents such as Vanguard, Charles Schwab and UBS who were quick to recognize this customer experience gap.

For each of the innovators above, the following holds true:

1. They identified a change in the way the market is operating and created a value proposition to address it
2. They delivered a new value proposition with a set of capabilities that focuses on customer experience and links the underlying products together
3. They constantly built and evolved an ecosystem to fuel and improve the new value proposition

More than just the experience, each of the above players realized that industry boundaries need to be transcended if they had to continue making progress.

So how can we define a new model of organizational design that is ready to meet the needs of the markets and customers we serve? The new model for CX focused org design is depicted in this illustration. As you can observe, the critical new element is the CX program which is guided by the connected communities.

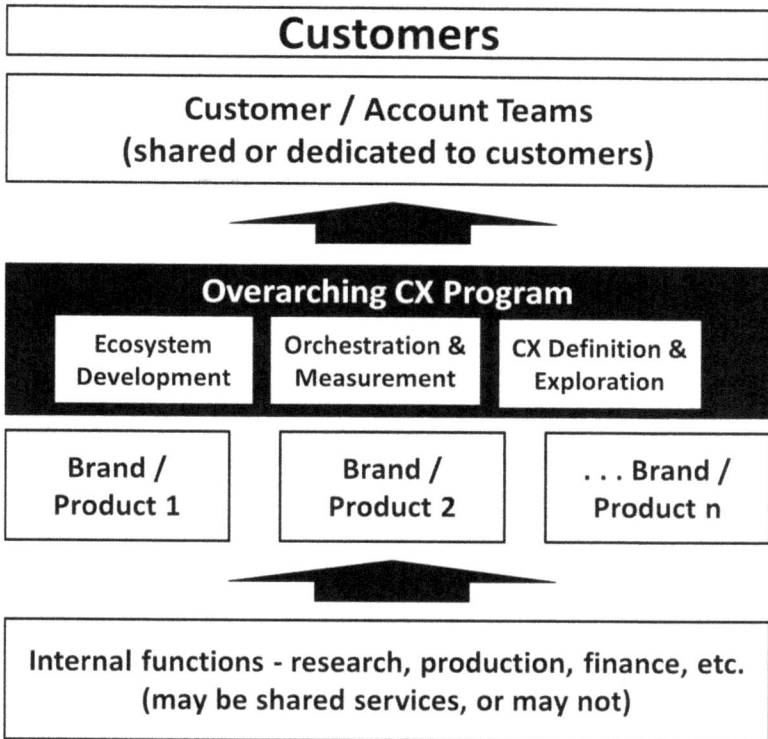

Customers

Customer / Account Teams (shared or dedicated to customers)

Overarching CX Program		
Ecosystem Development	Orchestration & Measurement	CX Definition & Exploration

Brand / Product 1	Brand / Product 2	. . . Brand / Product n

Internal functions - research, production, finance, etc. (may be shared services, or may not)

Fig: CX Focused Org Design

To be effective, the model will account for the following aspects:

1. Customer purpose driven customer experience programs
2. Ecosystem of industry players needed that are aligned to the purpose
3. Mechanisms to focus the products and brands to the top level customer experiences
4. Mechanisms to bring the customer experience to life

How do you define customer purpose? That's an important question because it is the first step in the journey towards creating a CX focused organizational design. Customer purpose is defined by looking at the customer and thinking about where and how your products fit into their overall experience. For example, health foods fit well with fitness programs and fitness centers, and they may also fit well with what nutritionists do. Similarly B2B firms should be looking at what their clients want to accomplish and how they are gearing up to help their clients meet those needs. The products take a back seat to this analysis because the strategy of the company is driven through an outside-in perspective. In fact, the product portfolio may undergo a dramatic shift as we prepare for the future. Think of IBM in the nineties when they slowly let go of their hardware business, or think of GE when they started to focus on software, or think of Amazon which forced Walmart and Barnes & Noble to adopt the product mix of the future.

There are many more examples that can be cited but I hope the core message is clear. We must focus on understanding the purpose of our customers that extends beyond our products, and organize around that. That means that our product mix will consist of products from other industry players too.

Creating such a design is not difficult. Operationalizing it is another matter. It is clear that connected customer experiences should be driving force for the organizations that hope to survive and thrive in the future. Every organization and every industry will move towards this reality. The only difference will be in how they move towards it.

So we now move on to the next and final step in this chapter on Execution. Let's now look at Connected Scorecards which will round up the discussion and will provide a full set of tools to meet the challenges of execution.

Connected Scorecard

We all know about the Balanced Scorecard. With experience come some lessons. The Balanced Scorecard and the associated tool called the Strategy Map were originally introduced by Dr. Robert Kaplan. Regardless of how extensively we use these tools, the concept is important to apply and understand, even at a high level. The strategy map alone gives tremendous food for thought. People and how they are motivated along the desired path are critical for a good org design. No amount of coaxing can accomplish what we don't or can't measure.

Moreover, the effectiveness of any methodology depends on what we feed into it. In this case, the primary input is the strategy or the way to play. I've introduced a simple, easy-to-use Connected Scorecard as an input to existent management methodologies such as the balanced scorecard. This scorecard brings the outside-in perspective to the top of the food chain. It provides a simple way to measure how we are achieving the goals of meeting the needs of our customers in a connected world.

The connected scorecard brings together everything we have discussed in book including CX, loyalty, customer engagement and integration. There are 2 core measurement groups in this scorecard:

1. Connected customer journeys
2. Ecosystem

The first one measures the breadth (how many) and depth (how well, financial contribution) of the customer journeys we are enabling. The second one measures how well we are including players in a cross industry fashion (coverage, relationship strength, competitive parity). Together these metrics will enable us to avoid the risk of simply paying lip service to this important evolution. The connected customer journeys will largely drive the ecosystem. But measuring the ecosystem can provide insights into the journeys as well.

The Connected Scorecard will hopefully mitigate the problems of isolated innovation, competitive inertia, and the issue of balancing the future with the present. It gives us a practical framework for driving and measuring our effectiveness in a connected world.

To make it easier to implement, it's best to think of the connected scorecard as an assess-recommend process. We assess the various dimensions, and the assessment should automatically give rise to recommendations.

Let's discuss these 2 components of the Connected Scorecard. It's meant to bring together everything in this book together to create a CX focused org powerhouse.

Dimension 1: Connected Customer Journeys

This dimension of the connected scorecard measures tangible progress on actual customer engagement. It forces us to create a top down and outside-in view of how we should be engaging our customers. Keep in mind from before that many different organizations from different organizations may participate in a connected customer journey, and it's not just limited to 2 organizations working with each other. In fact, the more partners from more industries the better.

The breadth metric of this dimension maps the customer journeys to the important business processes and channels. It gives immediate insight into whether we have brought in the forward thinking elements to the processes by considering the ecosystem components. It also outlines the financial or qualitative benefits we hope to realize. Some indicative questions that help us arrive at a good breadth metric are:

- How are we reaching customers outside the boundaries of our organization? Refer back to the ecosystem based CX we discussed in chapter one. The extended customer personas and customer journeys will provide us the input we need here. Both of them refer to how we can position our channel and supply partners as strategic partners jointly working to engage customers. This question also helps us think of aspects of the end to end customer journey that we lack. As we have seen, competition comes from unexpected sources. Just thinking of our own products leaves us vulnerable. We need to be looking at this closely to see how customers are meeting their needs, and whether those interactions lead customers away from us. In addition, analyzing this metric helps us check if our competition is adopting different methods to enter our customers' ecosystems in ways different from others.

- Do we know what customers want instead of relying on analytics? Refer back to the chapter on customer engagement which focused on creating one-one engagement with customers so we can personalize without invading privacy and without having to generalize. Think of tools such as interactive calculators, wish-lists etc.

- Do we have connected customer journeys across different functional processes? This question helps analyze if we are simply tackling a silo of the organization (e.g. customer acquisition), or are we able to cut across silos (acquisition, engagement, service).

The depth metric is where we actually realize the fruits of our connected efforts. This is where we understand if the goals we defined our being met, and provide tangible financial measurements. How well we execute defines how rapidly we get business units and product lines to engage full throttle. Research shows that the shelf life or management tolerance for innovation efforts in banks is about 18 months (see ref 16). My guess is that it is similar in other industries as well. So, the depth metric is important because it quantifies the items we set out to achieve.

Some indicative questions that help you define a good model for depth are:

- Do we see an increase in customer acquisition or retention? The true test of a customer journey is if it drives results. These can come in the form of new customers, more satisfied customers, less costs to service them, more profitable customers, and so on.
- Are we driving benefits both ways with the partners? In any partnership, especially in an ecosystem like this it is important to measure benefits we drive for our partners.
- Which partners or aspects of the customer journey are yielding more benefits than others? This is also critical to understand that some aspects of the customer journey will likely need more focus than others. This could simply arise because of customer preferences that we did not understand before, or that some behaviors simply need more time to change.

Dimension 2: Ecosystem

The work of connected communities and the effectiveness of the CX focused org design have to be measured. Being connected is the central premise of this book, and therefore how we play in the large needs spectrum of our customers is critical.

I've broken down the ecosystem into a few major categories. These should provide the basic building blocks of how we can begin to measure the ecosystem.

1. Coverage simply means the number and types of partners. It assesses the progress and initiatives we have that address end to end customer needs. It is meant to provide the answer to one simple question: How well are we looking from the outside-in? If you remember, the notion of Omni-Channel and enhancing our current channel capabilities through digital is important, but is inadequate for the future. In the future, we must look at connecting our products to what the customers do before and after they engage with us. The processes we should aim to cover will span across marketing, operations and service. And we'll take the connected customer journeys we created before and leverage them here to identify the right partners, and address the entire customer journey.

2. Relationship Strength will signify the depth of the partnership we establish. For example, we are all familiar with affiliate relationships. To create a true ecosystem, we need more than just affiliates. We need to address the customer journey jointly and help the customers meet their needs. So the coverage parameter will be qualified through the relationship strength measurement. Common

parameters to include here will be the extent of joint branding, data sharing, active conversations on customer engagement initiatives etc. A dormant ecosystem partnership is of little use.

3. Competitive parity helps us benchmark against emerging industry evolution. It's an excellent indicator of whether we are doing enough to strengthen and grow our position in the market. This analysis helps not only to validate our connected customer journeys, but it also helps us uncover new ones and decide to be a fast follower for something we may have missed. That's the nature of innovation. All ideas don't come to everyone.

The questions I mention here are may of course be different for different organizations and their use cases. The litmus test to validate them is to:

1. Ensure that an ecosystem is being leveraged
2. The ecosystem is being used as a true customer engagement partnership, not just as at arm's length as a supply partner, distribution partner or sales partner.
3. Benefits are being measured and reported both ways

Let's now briefly look at some examples of the connected scorecard to drive home the point, and make it easier to visualize what all of this means.

Scorecard in Action - Practical Scenarios

Based on the two dimensions, here's how the connected scorecard looks like in summary form. This is a template dashboard. For every company and strategic priority that will be new elements you might want to add.

Dimension	Measure	Question	Result
Connected Customer Journey	Breadth	Reaching customers outside our organizations?	A numeric scale can be defined for easy computation of combined score, and for comparison of various processes.
	Breadth	Knowing what customers want without analytics?	
	Breadth	Journeys across functional processes?	
	Depth	Are we seeing increased benefits?	
	Depth	Are our partners seeing benefits?	
Ecosystem	Coverage	Do we have partners from multiple industries?	
	Relationship strength	How well are we partnering?	
	Competitive Parity	Are we missing partnerships that competitors have?	

As our first example, consider a banking mobile app that customers use for transactions. Banks are increasingly making retailer offers available to their customers. Using the connected scorecard, we can see that this innovation has significant potential for improvement. I am including only the questions and results portion of the scorecard here for ease of use. Of course, these results are my outside assessment of this process as a consumer so should not be treated as an official assessment. It is meant as a sample to illustrate the connected scorecard.

Topic: Retail offers within banking mobile apps		
Question	Assessment	My Rating (1-5)
Reaching customers outside our organizations?	Little effort made to engage outside the bank's boundaries. It works for retailers as a distribution channel. There is minimal attempt by the bank or the retailer to jointly engage with customers.	1
Knowing what customers want without analytics?	There is little effort to engage customers in an exploration of their needs. These are available to use, if the customers choose.	1
Journeys across functional processes?	The offers are meant to spur spend, but are not thematic, not used for acquisition, for helping	2

	with financial advice, or for cross sell.	
Are we seeing increased benefits?	Without a doubt, there are benefits when it comes to spend if the customers use the offer. But the potential can be improved.	3
Are our partners seeing benefits?	Retailers will see benefits too in the form of new customer acquisition and for win-back. But the potential can be improved.	3
Do we have partners from multiple industries?	No, and we can improve the maturity if we include active partnerships with retailers directly.	1
How well are we partnering?	Only as channel partners through aggregator platforms. No real partnership exists.	1
Are we missing partnerships that competitors have?	No, all banks have similar levels of maturity. But there is significant potential to do more, and digital innovations are coming rapidly now.	1
	Overall score (average)	**1.8**

As we can see, the connected scorecard has provided quite a contrary view of this exciting innovation which is almost an industry on its own. There is a lot more that can be done. I'll leave that to the experts of course.

As another example, let's now consider the partnership between fitness providers and health insurers. We have covered the innovative partnership between Blue Cross Blue Shield of New Jersey and Lifetime Fitness. It's quite a beneficial partnership. I wouldn't want to analyze the specific partnership between BCBS of New Jersey and Lifetime Fitness. So let's apply the connected scorecard and see where we end up on the assessment of a generic partnership such as this. Of course, these results are my outside assessment of this process as a consumer so should not be treated as an official assessment. It is meant as a sample to illustrate the connected scorecard.

Topic: Health Insurers and Fitness providers		
Question	Assessment	My Rating (1-5)
Reaching customers outside our organizations?	Yes. The fitness provider definitely has the potential to acquire new customers. I have not seen models where existing fitness customers are being sent to health insurers. This could be a challenge to implement for customers insured by corporate plans but additional revenue models can be created.	2
Knowing what customers want	I haven't seen mature models yet where	2

without analytics?	customers are being guided on the basis of their health or related needs. That might also alleviate the privacy and data sharing concerns.	
Journeys across functional processes?	So far, the journeys are limited because they are hands off and focus on potential claims reduction through incentives on fitness. These could be more hands on through more proactive health management, fitness activities, social recognition, etc.	1
Are we seeing increased benefits?	This particular partnership has benefits to insurers by way of lower claims.	3
Are our partners seeing benefits?	Fitness center gain too by way of new customers and also win-back of customers.	3
Do we have partners from multiple industries?	Yes, but there is potential to do a lot more. Right now, the focus is on fitness. But diet still is unaddressed. Potential partnerships with retailers may help. Also, alternative	1

	medicine may have a role to play as well. Medical practitioners such as independent dieticians and health coaches may be included as well. Social activities such as marathons can also be considered part of the ecosystem.	
How well are we partnering?	The partners are at an arm's length. Regulatory concerns are slowing the evolution but there is much more that can be done without regulatory fallout.	1
Are we missing partnerships that competitors have?	Not at this time, but there is significant potential	2
	Overall score (average)	**2.1**

As is evident, the connected scorecard has provided insights into not only this specific features but also how new innovations can create additional revenue streams for insurers and fitness centers. In addition, the social motivations of members can also be satisfied. There is so much more that can be done. I'll leave that to the experts of course.

Let's take one final example and consider the travel and hospitality industry with the example of an aggregator (such as hotels.com) and a hotel. As before, I am taking a generic example and not commenting on any specific organization or partnership. Of course, these results are my outside assessment of this process as a consumer so should not be treated as an official assessment. It is meant as a sample to illustrate the connected scorecard.

Topic: Hotel aggregator sites & hotels		
Question	**Assessment**	**My Rating (1-5)**
Reaching customers outside our organizations?	Yes, but this is a typical channel distribution partnership.	1
Knowing what customers want without analytics?	No engagement of customers based on their aspirations and plans. Aggregators may implements win back strategies with context of previous searches but there are no other efforts to personalize.	1
Journeys across functional processes?	The journeys are limited to acquisition alone. As we saw in the first question, this is also not a true customer engagement partnership	1
Are we seeing increased benefits?	Yes, the aggregator makes commissions, and the hotel acquires customers.	1
Are our partners	Yes, the aggregator makes	2

seeing benefits?	commissions, and the hotel acquires customers.	
Do we have partners from multiple industries?	No, but there is significant potential to include insurance, travel planners, local providers, taxis etc.	1
How well are we partnering?	The partnership is at an arm's length. No real integration except the processes required to fulfil transactions.	1
Are we missing partnerships that competitors have?	No, but there is significant scope for improvement if we consider the purpose customers have when they visit either the aggregator or the hotel	1
	Overall score (average)	**1.1**

Once again, an assessment based on the connected scorecard opens us up to possibilities that are not immediately visible. It also opens up a strategic conversation on how the players should meet the purpose of customers, rather than just fulfilling the transaction they came to the providers for. I'll leave the detailed roadmap development to the experts of course.

Summary

I included this chapter because it is perhaps the most important aspect of innovation. Even if we can execute imperfectly but still deliver the benefits in a limited way, it will still be a big step forward towards staying relevant in a connected world. The notion of an ecosystem based, customer purpose focused partnership is not far from realization. Companies are doing it already in various ways. Digital wallets, voice activated assistants, and chabots on our messaging platforms are all attempts in this direction. The window of opportunity will not last for long however. The pace and nature of technology is no longer about scale and compute power waiting to be leveraged or harnessed. The power is in customers' hands already, or is being placed there every day. Behaviors are being conditioned and set rapidly.

Thinking about the customer journeys we want to enable, and gearing up to execute with agility is more critical than it was till just a decade so. Why is that? It's simply because the pace of change is causing well defined industry boundaries to crumble rapidly. And that's the reason I outlined the concept of Connected Communities to set the charter and innovate without being hampered by the inertia of the current business. This connected layer should also be inserted subsequently in the formal organizational structure to ensure that customer experiences are driven according to the connected charter. Finally, the connected scorecard will consistently and holistically measure the progress on the connected company charter. These are all formal constructs, because the time is ripe for transformation, and that journey cannot be undertaken from the outside.

BLOCK 5: EXECUTION

CONCLUSION

If you've come this far, you've seen how the various elements of being a connected company (see ref 41) culminate in the connected scorecard. The scorecard makes everything come alive. It helps create discipline around a type of innovation the industry has not seen before. So much so that previous management theories and models are only partially relevant for the future. We touched upon a few of them such as the Innovators Dilemma (see ref 37) and the ambidextrous organization (see ref 8). We discussed how these need to be expanded in context of a connected world.

The biggest area of focus that we need to address is that our vision and strategy has to look beyond our own products and services. The customer journeys we develop must transcend the boundaries of multiple industry players. Our loyalty models need to move towards aspirations. Our partnerships should become more than just about fulfilling channel sales, distribution, or supply needs. And finally, the ecosystems we create should be constantly expanded as our view of the customer purpose evolves.

Needless to say, innovation as per an ecosystem will not come easy. It needs resilience and doing something new. We can take inspiration from companies that are already innovating at breakneck speed. However, technology and changing dynamics of the workforce are in favor of those who will adapt their innovation journeys to fit the context of ecosystems. Ecosystems will beat individual propositions. This was not so till only a few years ago. Due to the rise of the shared economy, everywhere you see there are innovators ready to offer us a service to fulfil a need. Think of any business, even healthcare, and intelligent applications of technology innovation are demolishing the advantages that were being taken for granted. New business models being created are putting the customer at the center of the conversation. This change in business focus is creating new opportunities that were visible previously but left untapped.

I hope you've started to think of how the platforms we are building today will be more useful if they talk to other platforms. The individual platforms we are building to keep customers engaged will soon become of limited utility. That's because the power of the connected ecosystem will allow for much better choice, much more personalization, and multiple entry points into the customer experience. A connected ecosystem will be able to not only personalize, but also do it at a level that will raise the engagement to an aspirational level of loyalty.

This is not to say that we should not aim to build a platform of our own. It's extremely important to do that of course. The crucial difference in approach will be to plug into other platforms so we can create a multiple industry ecosystem. The expanded platform will cater to the extended customer persona.

The expansion of the ecosystem will be limited only by our imagination and effort. It can start small with the obvious use cases, and then expand over time to meet customer needs as they evolve. The expansion will depend on how well participants in the ecosystem can share data, and how well they can help each other engage customers thematically. And most importantly, the participants in the ecosystem cannot look at other constituents as channel partners. Doing so will be same old wine in a new bottle. The idea would be engage with the extended customer persona as a unified company.

At the end, I want to leave you with 2 things. First, if you are looking for what customer engagement is, you've found it. It is external reinforcement and interaction as per an ecosystem. We developed an equation for it as well (see chapter 3 for the equation). Second, the core of all innovation stems from looking at the customers as people and thinking of how to make their lives better. That's how we started – developing extended customer personas and connected customer journeys. And we ended with the connected scorecard to help align the execution.

Now go!

CONCLUSION

REFERENCES

1. The HorizonbFit program -
   https://members.horizonbfit.com/horizonbfitmobile#.
   The program is powered by Advanta Health
   Solutions.
2. Alfa-Bank, with its save more when you move
   program. http://activity.alfabank.ru/Activity/
3. Plenti, the multi-retailer and cross industry loyalty
   program by American Express.
   https://www.americanexpress.com/us/credit-
   cards/card/plenti/
4. COLLOQUY: An average household uses only 30% of
   the loyalty programs they are signed up in.
   https://www.colloquy.com/latest-news/2015-colloquy-
   loyalty-census/
5. Report on loyalty by Capgemini Consulting:
   https://www.capgemini.com/resources/fixing-the-
   cracks-reinventing-loyalty-programs-for-the-digital-
   age

6. The Bond Brand Loyalty report – 44% of customers feel that it is easy to replace the rewards program, http://info.bondbrandloyalty.com/hubfs/Resources/Bond_Brand_Loyalty_2015_Loyalty_Report.pdf

7. Effect of Customer-centric structure on long term financial performance – Lee, Sridhar, Henderson, Palmatier. http://www.msi.org/reports/effect-of-customer-centric-structure-on-firm-performance/

8. Ambidextrous organizations - HBR - https://hbr.org/2004/04/the-ambidextrous-organization

9. Putting The Balanced scorecard To Work - https://hbr.org/1993/09/putting-the-balanced-scorecard-to-work

10. How to acquire profitable customers: https://warrington.ufl.edu/centers/retailcenter/docs/papers/Lewis2004.pdf

11. Field experiments in trust and brand consideration - http://web.mit.edu/hauser/www/Hauser%20Articles/Liberali_Urban_Hauser_competitive%20information%20IJRM%202013.pdf

12. MIT paper on Trust imperative - http://ebusiness.mit.edu/research/papers/175_Urban_Trust.pdf

13. Customer loyalty is fleeting: https://thefinancialbrand.com/51081/banking-big-data-opportunity/

14. Millennials find banks irrelevant - https://thefinancialbrand.com/37787/millennial-banking-survey-viacom/

15. Millennials find banks irrelevant - http://www.millennialdisruptionindex.com/

16. 18 months for innovation in banking - Innovation and the Future Proof Bank: A Practical Guide to Doing Different, James A Gardner, http://www.wiley.com/WileyCDA/WileyTitle/productCd-0470714190.html

17. Solving the warranty problem for consumer using Blockchain, https://www2.deloitte.com/nl/nl/pages/deloitte-digital/artikelen/warranty-solution-based-on-blockchain.html

18. How Wells Fargo is integrating with Xero to make life easier for small businesses and entrepreneurs, https://www.wellsfargo.com/about/press/2016/new-dataexchange-method_0607/

19. How to help your customers engage with you on Facebook Messenger, https://developers.facebook.com/blog/post/2016/04/12/bots-for-messenger/

20. How UK is pushing for bank interoperability through its PSD2 regulation, https://www.gov.uk/government/consultations/implementation-of-the-revised-eu-payment-services-directive-psdii

21. PayPal, Visa and MasterCard enter into agreements to open up business for each other, https://www.bloomberg.com/news/articles/2016-07-21/paypal-and-visa-end-battle-unveiling-pact-on-fees-and-data

22. Facebook impacts the importance of business pages and fans, https://www.facebook.com/business/news/update-to-facebook-news-feed

23. New FinTech innovations to target millennials and passive savers, http://www.barrons.com/articles/two-new-mobile-investing-apps-for-millennials-1453527209

24. What is a Robo-Advisor, http://www.investopedia.com/terms/r/roboadvisor-roboadviser.asp

25. Multi-sided platforms and the Fidor example, http://www.causeit.org/multi-sided-platforms-and-the-fidor-example/

26. What is blockchain technology, https://blockgeeks.com/guides/what-is-blockchain-technology/

27. The value of keeping the right customers, https://hbr.org/2014/10/the-value-of-keeping-the-right-customers

28. What went wrong at J. C. Penney? http://hbswk.hbs.edu/item/what-went-wrong-at-j-c-penney

29. Banks must differentiate, https://thefinancialbrand.com/51778/millennial-bank-switching-study/

30. A Thousand Tribes: How Technology Unites People in Great Companies, https://www.amazon.com/Thousand-Tribes-Technology-Unites-Companies/dp/0471222836

31. Walgreens links healthy choices with rewards and loyalty, https://www.walgreens.com/steps/brhc-loggedout.jsp

32. Will the sharing economy disrupt trucking, https://www.trucks.com/2016/08/24/sharing-economy-trucking-transportation/

33. Can we regulate Bitcoin, https://www.wired.com/2016/03/must-understand-bitcoin-regulate/

34. How millennials will transform industry, http://www.millennialdisruptionindex.com/

35. What is NPS? http://www.netpromotersystem.com/about/index.aspx

36. Accelerate! (XLR8), Book, https://www.kotterinternational.com/book/accelerate/

37. The Innovators Dilemma, Clayton Christensen, http://web.mit.edu/6.933/www/Fall2000/teradyne/clay.html

38. Wearables down but not out, http://www.marketwatch.com/story/the-wearable-craze-isnt-dead-yet-2017-01-31

39. Pressure in food cereal category,
    http://www.foodbusinessnews.net/articles/news_home
    /Business_News/2016/12/Pressure_in_cereal_category_
    pr.aspx

40. How connected devices are affecting brands and
    established channels, https://evrythng.com/why-
    amazon-dash-is-a-threat-to-brands-and-how-they-can-
    fight-back/

41. The Connected Company,
    http://manishgrover.com/connected-company-
    framework/

<u>Go Online!</u>

Use the below QR code to go to the book website and also access the list of references online:

<u>http://www.manishgrover.com/connected</u>

REFERENCES

ABOUT THE AUTHOR

@manishgrover | www.manishgrover.com

I could say that I am a strategist, marketer, manager, leader or consultant, but that would exclude my other identities of father, son, entrepreneur, engineer, consumer, student, blogger, coach, biker, musician (aspiring), chef (decent) and among many others, a dreamer.

Should I choose a professional label, or a personal one? It depends on the context, I guess. So I'll leave it to you.

Enjoy the book. It's my view of the future of customer engagement. Connect with me @ www.manishgrover.com

Manish Grover | *MBA (Carnegie Mellon)* | *MS (Florida Atlantic)* | *BE Honors (BITS Pilani)*